MORE PRAISE FOR *THE SILENT LANGUAGE OF LEADERS*

"Learn to align your verbal and non-verbal communication and you are on your way to becoming a better leader. *The Silent Language of Leaders* is the only book you need to bring yourself up to speed."

—**Karen Tucker**, CEO, Churchill Club

"Successful business executives understand and achieve higher levels of effectiveness when their words are in sync with their body language. Carol Kinsey Goman's new book showcases the important body language techniques needed to build trust in a rapidly changing world. Savvy executives will use her recommendations immediately to build stronger relationships, shape perceptions, and get results."

—**Lee Hornick**, program director, The Conference Board, and president, Business Communications Worldwide, Inc.

"This book is an outstanding resource to help managers at all levels become better communicators and leaders."

—**Shirley Gaufin**, chief human resources officer, Black & Veatch Corporation

"Whether it's in front of an individual or a large group, communication is a key component of your leadership success. And a major aspect of that success is your body language. This silent method of communication can be deadly if you don't know the signals that you are sending. Carol Kinsey Goman provides a guidebook to help you navigate this complex aspect of leadership."

—**Jon Peters**, president, The Institute for Management Studies

"People don't realize how their true strengths and weaknesses are revealed by their body language. Carol Kinsey Goman's observations and insights are unique."

—**Charles Lynch**, chairman, Market Value Partners

THE SILENT LANGUAGE of LEADERS

HOW BODY LANGUAGE CAN HELP —OR HURT—HOW YOU LEAD

CAROL KINSEY GOMAN

JOSSEY-BASS
A Wiley Imprint
www.josseybass.com

Published by Jossey-Bass
A Wiley Imprint
989 Market Street, San Francisco, CA 94103-1741—www.josseybass.com

Jossey-Bass books and products are available through most bookstores. To contact Jossey-Bass directly call our Customer Care Department within the U.S. at 800-956-7739, outside the U.S. at 317-572-3986, or fax 317-572-4002.

Jossey-Bass also publishes its books in a variety of electronic formats. Some content that appears in print may not be available in electronic books.

Library of Congress Cataloging-in-Publication Data

Goman, Carol Kinsey.
  The silent language of leaders : how body language can help—or hurt—how you lead / Carol Kinsey Goman. – 1st ed.
        p. cm.
    Includes bibliographical references and index.
    ISBN 978-0-470-87636-7 (hardback)
1. Body language. 2. Nonverbal communication in the workplace.
3. Communication in management. 4. Leadership. 5. Communication in organizations.
I. Title.
  BF637.N66G664 2011
  650.1′3–dc22

                                                              2010050248

Printed in the United States of America
FIRST EDITION
HB Printing   10 9 8 7 6 5 4 3

CONTENTS

Contents

Contents

Contents

THE
SILENT
LANGUAGE
of LEADERS

INTRODUCTION

The Leadership–Body Language Connection

Leadership is about communication. You already know that. So, in preparing for an important meeting, you concentrate on what to say, you memorize crucial points, and you rehearse your presentation so that you will come across as credible and convincing.

But did you also know that the people you're speaking to will have subliminally evaluated your credibility, confidence, likeability, and trustworthiness in the first seven seconds—before you had a chance to deliver your well-rehearsed speaking points? Did you know that your use of personal space, physical gestures, posture, facial expressions, and eye contact could already have sabotaged your message? And, most critically, did you know that any time your words and body language were

1

out of alignment, people believed what they saw and not what you said?

So, if you went into that important meeting with all the right words and all the wrong moves, you probably left sensing that things didn't go as well as you'd hoped. But you might not know why.

Leadership is also about building and sustaining positive relationships. You know that too. You travel to meet personally with key customers, go out with coworkers to get to know them better, arrange "town hall" meetings in order to interact more closely with frontline workers.

But did you know that your ability to accurately read and respond to the body language of others is fundamental to building empathy and rapport? If you misinterpreted and ignored important nonverbal signals from your colleagues, customers, or employees, you probably parted company feeling vaguely dissatisfied with the relationship you'd established, again not knowing why, but realizing something needed to be done about it.

That's when you might hire me.

I get paid to stalk leaders.

Well, not literally, but that is how one of my satisfied clients humorously described my services.

I'm a professional communicator, the author of eleven business books, and an international keynote speaker. But when I'm not traveling around the world on speaking engagements, I coach people like you—managers, team leaders, entrepreneurs, and senior executives who are looking for ways to become even more effective in their ability to relate with and influence others.

So, I stalk—more accurately, "shadow"—these leaders, observing them as they run meetings, interact informally with employees and colleagues, consult with customers, negotiate business deals, and make formal presentations.

OH, THE THINGS I'VE SEEN!

Body language is the management of time, space, appearance, posture, gesture, vocal prosody, touch, smell, facial expression, and eye contact. The latest research in neuroscience and psychology has proven that body language is crucial to leadership effectiveness—and this book will show you exactly how it impacts a leader's ability to negotiate, manage change, build trust, project charisma, and promote collaboration. But my interest in body language started long before I gave speeches or coached leaders. In training for my previous occupation as a therapist in private practice, I learned to pay close attention to nonverbal signals. In doing so, I became aware of the way body language can underscore what a person is saying, but can also undermine or even contradict it. When very relaxed, people had certain ways of entering my office and certain physical positions that they assumed. But when they were concerned or unconvinced, their postures and expressions changed dramatically. I also saw that quite often their body language was in direct opposition to their words, and I learned to trust the subliminal messages from their bodies as much as, or more than, their verbal responses. Soon it became second nature to "decode" body language cues and to use what I discovered to help people overcome internal resistance and to reinforce personal motivation in order to make positive changes in their lives.

When I started to coach organizational leaders, I was surprised to find how unfamiliar businesspeople were with nonverbal communication. For the past twenty years, I've studied and been awed by the impact of body language on leadership results. I've seen firsthand how nonverbal signals can literally make or break a leader's success. I also saw that most leaders were nonverbally illiterate—completely out of touch with the effect their body language had on others and unaware of the clear nonverbal signals that were being sent by clients and colleagues in every business encounter. The human brain is hardwired to read and respond to these signals, but most leaders don't know that the process is taking place and are unequipped, therefore, to use it to their advantage.

THE TIME IS RIGHT

It's a great time to start building your nonverbal intelligence. In fact, your timing couldn't be better. Three factors have come together to put body language skills at the top of a leader's to-do list: (1) the visual technology revolution, (2) advances in scientific research that provide direct links between body language and leadership results, and (3) the growing importance of cross-cultural communication with the global workforce.

The Visual Technology Revolution

Smile—you're on someone's camera! From YouTube postings to cell phones with video capability to image-driven social media, there is no escaping the visual technology revolution. And we are only beginning to see the impact of this revolution on businesses around the world.

Cisco System's TelePresence is only one example of a number of new products geared for the workplace. This new generation of videoconferencing technology allows people in different locations to meet as though they were face-to-face, with high-definition video and audio streaming in real time, no matter what the distance.

Technological advances will continue to revolutionize the way enterprises, employees, and consumers communicate and interact. As multimedia applications become increasingly utilized and integrated, users will demand to be able to access these applications wherever they are and on any device, just as they do voice and data. For example, in the future, the ability to set up a Cisco TelePresence session will be as easy and as commonplace as making a phone call is today.

Science, Leadership, and Body Language

Research by the MIT Media Lab shows the ways that subtle nonverbal cues provide powerful signals about what's really going on in a business interaction.[1] For example, whether you win or lose a negotiation is strongly influenced by unconscious factors, such as the way your body postures match those of the other person, the level of physical activity as you talk, and the degree to which one of you sets the tone—literally—of the conversation. Through the use of devices (called Sociometers) that monitor and analyze patterns of unconscious social signals passing between people, researchers with no knowledge of a conversation's content can predict the outcome of a negotiation, a presentation of a business plan, or a job interview in the first two minutes of that interaction.

But nothing has contributed more to the scientific validity of reading body language than neuroscience and the use of functional magnetic resonance imaging (fMRI). Magnetic resonance imaging (MRI) uses radio waves and a strong magnetic field to take clear and detailed pictures of internal organs and tissues. FMRI applies this technology to identifying regions of the brain where blood vessels are expanding, chemical changes are taking place, or extra oxygen is being delivered.

FMRI has been held up as a breakthrough technology for better understanding the brain, and it has added great credibility to nonverbal communication. Consider, for example, the research from Duke University that shows why we like and remember those who smile at us: using fMRI, the Duke researchers found that the orbitofrontal cortices (a "reward center" in the brain) were more active when subjects were learning and recalling the names of smiling individuals.[2]

Global Workforce

The tricky thing about body language is that we are often unaware of how we are reacting to it. We may form a negative opinion about someone because he slouches, won't look us in the eye (or looks too intently), or stands too close to us when he speaks. Because we are unaware of how or why we made the judgment, we are unable to filter out our biases. And nowhere is this problem more evident than when we are reacting to nonverbal communication from people in different cultures.

I'll discuss approaches to this problem later in the book, but remember for now that your success as a leader will depend increasingly on your ability to get top business results with a multinational workforce—not just because participating in global teams is fast becoming part of your job description, but also because the workforce within your own national borders is growing more and more diverse, ethnically and culturally, every day. Understanding the similarities and accommodating the differences in multicultural body language are key elements of this success.

CHAPTER OUTLINE

You picked up this book because you realize (or suspect) that nonverbal communication can be used to your leadership advantage. I wrote *The Silent Language of Leaders* to give savvy leaders like you that nonverbal "edge." This book is unlike any other body language book on the market. It speaks directly to leadership situations you face every day and offers insights and practical strategies for those situations to help you become an even more effective communicator and leader.

This book presents a key leadership strategy in an engaging and pragmatic way. Throughout the book you'll find real-life leadership examples and effective body language suggestions for a variety of workplace situations—along with the latest scientific research that backs them up. Here's a brief overview.

Chapter One, Leadership at a Glance, lays a frame-work for the book by giving an overview of the importance of body language to leadership success. It covers your personal "curb appeal"—the first impression people have of you, the nonverbal signals that are most important for leadership, the mistakes people make reading you, and why the key to effective body language is in the eye of the beholder.

Following this introductory overview, the next three chapters highlight the power of body language in crucial aspects of leadership and show you how to harness that power. Each chapter explains what other people are telling you with their nonverbal signals, and each offers strategies for adjusting your own body language for maximum effect.

Chapter Two, Negotiation, covers the nonverbal intelligence you need in a negotiation. It includes tips on reading the body language responses of your counterpart, how to project comfort and credibility, how to make a positive impression in the first seven seconds, how to use power cues to regain the upper hand, and what body language can tell you about candor and deception. Chapter Three, Leading Change, looks at how to use body language to minimize resistance and build employee commitment to organizational transformation. It gives you guidelines for making formal change announcements and explores the power of emotion (emotional contagion, emotional overflow, emotional suppression) and why it is so difficult to hide what you feel. Then it asks (and answers) the intriguing question: Can you fake charisma? Chapter Four, Collaboration, looks at the body language of inclusion and motivation. It highlights the importance of eye contact and the use of "mirroring" to make everyone on the team feel valued. It explains why your paralinguistics (how you say what you say) are so important, why it matters where you sit in a meeting, and what your office says about you as a collaborative leader. Chapter Five, Communicating Virtually and Face-to-Face, examines what brain research tells us about body language in the digital age. It covers the use of nonverbal communication in virtual environments, the advantages of face-to-face meetings, and why the impact of some body language signals is greater in a videoconference than in person.

Chapter Six, He Leads, She Leads, deals with gender differences in body language and how these differences impact male and female leadership effectiveness. In this chapter you'll learn the body language strengths and weaknesses that men and women bring to their leadership roles and what both can learn about communicating more effectively.

Chapter Seven, Working with Global Teams, examines which body language signals are universal and which are culturally determined. You'll discover why body language that feels so right in one culture may be ineffective or even offensive in another. *The Silent Language of Leaders* is also the first body language book to feature a global panel of professionals commenting on the impact of nonverbal communication, and Chapter Eight, International Body Language, is written from this multinational viewpoint. In it, twelve global communicators give cross-cultural and nonverbal business advice to visiting executives.

Chapter Nine, The Nonverbal Future of Leadership, takes a look at the values and expectations of the newest generation of workers, the coming advances in communication technologies, a new model for leadership—and how all these factors will combine to make body language skills even more crucial for leaders in the future.

FROM GOOD TO OUTSTANDING

I am occasionally hired by an organization to coach an underperforming leader, but I most often coach leaders who are already good at their jobs. And I love the process of working with smart, talented, and motivated professionals and watching them achieve outstanding leadership results.

When properly used, body language can be your key to greater success. It can help you develop positive business relationships, influence and motivate the people who report to you, improve productivity, bond with members of your team, present your ideas with more impact, work effectively in a multicultural world, and project your personal brand of charisma. It is a "secret weapon" that many great leaders have learned to use to their advantage. Now you can too!

1
LEADERSHIP AT A GLANCE

How People Read the Body Language of Leaders

The senior vice president of a Fortune 500 company is speaking at a leadership conference in New York. He's a polished presenter with an impressive selection of organizational "war stories" delivered with a charming, self-deprecating sense of humor. The audience likes him. They like him a lot.

Then, as he finishes his comments, he folds his arms across his chest and says, "I'm open for questions. Please, ask me anything."

At this point, there is a noticeable shift of energy in the room—from engagement to uncertainty. The audience that was so attentive only moments ago is now somehow unable to think of anything to ask.

I was at that event. As one of the speakers scheduled to follow the executive, I was seated at a table onstage with a clear view of the entire room. And the minute I saw that single gesture, I knew exactly how the audience would react.

Later I talked with the speaker (who didn't realize he'd crossed his arms) and interviewed members of the audience (none of whom recalled the arm movement, but all of whom remembered struggling to come up with a question).

So what happened? How could a simple gesture that none of the participants were even aware of have had such a potent impact? This chapter will answer that question, first by explaining two things: (1) how the human brain processes verbal and nonverbal communication, and (2) how the early origins of body language "wired" us for certain predictable responses. As promised in the introduction, this chapter offers an expanded overview of the importance of body language to leadership success: it will explain why the key to effective body language is to view it through the eye of the beholder; it will help you evaluate your personal "curb appeal"—the first impression people have of you; it will introduce you to the two sets of non-verbal signals that followers look for in leaders. And last but not least, it will alert you to the most common mistakes people make reading your body language.

YOUR THREE BRAINS

Although neuroscience has advanced substantially in recent years, there is still controversy about the precise functions of the various brain structures. So it may be overly simplistic, but helpful, to think of the human brain is as if it were three brains: the ancient reptilian brain, the cortical brain, and the limbic brain.

The reptilian brain, the oldest of the three brain systems, consists of the brain stem and cerebellum. It controls the body's vital functions, such as heart rate, breathing, body temperature, and balance. Because the reptilian brain is primarily concerned with physical survival, it plays a crucial role in reproduction, social dominance, and establishing and defending territory. The behaviors it generates are instinctive, automatic, and highly resistant to change.

The cortical brain (with its two large cerebral hemispheres) is the newest system of the brain and the seat of our conscious thought. The prefrontal cortex acts as the "executive" for the brain. It handles such activities as language, analysis, and strategizing. We use the cortical brain when organizing our thoughts, setting goals, making plans, and solving complex problems. In the cortical system, the left brain hemisphere controls the right side of the body, and the right brain hemisphere controls the left side of the body. The hemispheres also have different specialties: the left is typically responsible for language, logic, and math; the right specializes in spatial concepts, music, visual imagery, and facial recognition. The two hemispheres communicate with one another by way of a thick band made up of nerve fibers called the corpus callosum.

The limbic brain is in the middle of the reptilian and cortical brains (both in terms of evolution and physical location). It includes the amygdala, hippocampus, cingulated gyrus, orbital frontal cortex, and insula. The limbic system, in particular the amygdala (an almond-shaped region that is located just in front of the hippocampus), is the first part of the brain to receive emotional information and react to it. As such, the amygdala acts as the "alarm system" for the brain, taking in all incoming stimuli (both physical and psychological) to decide whether or not they are threatening. It tends to become aroused in proportion to the strength of an emotional response—and the arousal to danger comes on faster and with far more intensity than the arousal to a potential reward.

In business, as in our social lives, emotions are the key drivers in decision making. Our logical processes are often only rational justifications for emotional decisions. And because most emotional decisions are made without conscious deliberation, they impact us with the immediacy and power of a limbic-brain imperative—unconsidered, unannounced, and, in most cases, impossible to resist. The limbic brain is most responsible for value judgments (often based on emotional reactions to body language cues) that strongly influence our reactions and behaviors.

It is also the limbic brain that plays the key role in nonverbal communication, in both generating and interpreting body language—a fact that explains why so many body language signals are the same around the world. An employee spots a friend, and immediately her eyebrows raise and her eyes widen in recognition; a team member reacts to distressful news by caving in his upper body and lowering his head; the winner of a conference door prize touches the base of her neck in surprise and delight; an executive's lips compress when pressured to answer an unwelcome question. All of these nonverbal limbic responses can be seen whether you are in São Paulo, Singapore, or San Francisco.

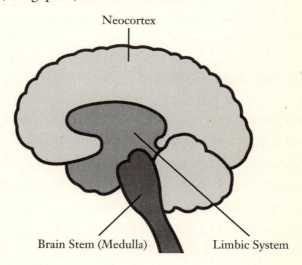

Neocortex

Brain Stem (Medulla)   Limbic System

The triune brain

Research by John-Dylan Haynes and his team at the Center for Neuroscience in Berlin used functional magnetic resonance imaging (fMRI) scans to demonstrate that they could tell what test subjects were going to do as early as ten seconds before the subjects were aware that they had made up their minds. This study showed that unconscious predictive brain activity comes first, and the conscious experience follows.[1]

In the case of the conference speaker, although his words commanded the audience's conscious attention, his gesture spoke distinctly, but covertly, to their limbic brains. Because his words and gesture were out of alignment, the audience became confused and unsettled. And when we humans are faced with conflicting verbal and nonverbal messages, we will almost always believe and react to the nonverbal message. Why? Because we have been "wired" that way.

WIRED FOR BODY LANGUAGE

Human beings are genetically programmed to look for nonverbal cues and to quickly understand their meaning. Body language was the basis for our earliest form of communication when the split-second ability to recognize whether a person or situation was benign or dangerous was often a matter of life or death.

Of course, many aspects of body language are culturally determined. (More about this in Chapter Eight.) But whether our knowledge is innate or learned at an early age, by the time we are adults we have a full vocabulary of nonverbal signals that we instinctively read in others and automatically react to—even if they have no validity in a contemporary context.

For example: in our prehistory, it may have been vitally important to see an approaching person's hands in order to evaluate his intent. If hands were concealed, they could very well be holding a rock, a club, or other means of doing us harm. In a business meeting today, with no logical reason to do so, we still instinctively mistrust someone who keeps his hands out of sight—in his pockets, below the table, or behind his back.

The Biology of Body Language

For insight into the body language of pride and shame, scientists studied the behaviors of athletes participating in judo matches at the 2004 Olympic and Paralympic Games. The competitors represented thirty countries, including Algeria, Taiwan, Ukraine, and the United States. The research report in the journal *Proceedings of the National Academy of Sciences* stated that body language of blind and sighted athletes showed the same patterns. The researchers' conclusion was that because congenitally blind individuals could not have learned the nonverbal aspects of pride and shame from watching others, these displays of victory or defeat are likely to be innate biological responses that have evolved over time.[2]

THE EYE OF THE BEHOLDER

Back to our conference speaker. Why do you suppose he made such a "closed" gesture just as he was asking the audience to open up? There could have been several reasons. He might have been more comfortable standing this way. He might have been cold. The gesture might have been one he used habitually to help him think whenever questioned. Or maybe he was actually reluctant to interact with the audience.

But I never asked him that question because "why" didn't matter.

It never does.

What does matter (at least to me as a coach) is helping you understand how your expressions, gestures, eye contact, use of space, postures, and all the other aspects of nonverbal communication will most likely be interpreted by others—and how those interpretations will most likely affect the observers' behavior.

Your audience will most likely be unaware of when and how it sensed as a group that "something wasn't quite right"—or, conversely, that it could now safely place its trust in you. The decision, however, would rarely if ever have been based on a critical analysis of your statements. It would, instead, have been based on an intuitive assessment of what your audience believed you really meant by those statements (the intentions, motivations, and agenda underlying them). This information would have been communicated nonverbally and evaluated by primitive emotional reactions that have changed very little since cavemen first began grunting incoherently at one another.

This fact is crucial to the use of body language for leadership success, so let me say it again: *body language is in the eye of the beholder*. The impact of your nonverbal communication lies in what others believe you intend and how that perception guides their reactions.

PERSONAL CURB APPEAL

In *The Political Brain*, a wonderful book about the role of emotion in politics, Drew Westen talks about curb appeal. Of course, Westen is referring to personal curb appeal. According to Westen: "One of the main determinants of electoral success is simply a candidate's curb appeal. Curb appeal is the feeling voters get when they 'drive by' a candidate a few times on television and form an emotional impression."[3]

What Westen found was that, after party affiliation, the most important predictor of how people vote is their emotional reaction (gut feeling) toward the candidate. For years now, I've been finding identical reactions in the workplace. A long time before your performance proves them right or wrong, people will have made an emotional decision about whether to follow you, trust you, or even listen to you. So the question I ask all my clients is "What is your personal curb appeal?" How do employees, team members, customers, and colleagues feel about you when they "drive by" your office a few times or observe you in the corporate hallways?

Research shows that your personal curb appeal can be assessed quickly and that many times these instant assessments are startlingly accurate. Psychologists Nalini Ambady and Robert Rosenthal conducted experiments involving what they called "thin slices of behavior."[4] These studies have been referenced in numerous writings—most famously, in Malcolm Gladwell's book *Blink*. In one such study, subjects watched a thirty-second clip of college teachers at the beginning of a term and rated them on such characteristics as accepting, active, competent, and confident. Analyzing this small sampling of behaviors, raters were able to accurately predict how students would evaluate those same teachers at the end of the course.

As you would suspect, thin slicing is primarily a nonverbal process. When Ambady and Rosenthal turned off the audio portion of the teachers' video clip, so that subjects had to rely only on body language cues, the accuracy of their predictions remained just as high.

The Look of Leadership

The major issue of the first televised presidential debate (in 1960) became the photogenic appeal of John F. Kennedy versus the sickly look of his opponent, Richard Nixon.

Several factors contributed to Nixon's poor image. His ill health leading up to the debate, which resulted in a drastic weight loss. His refusal to wear makeup despite the pallid complexion caused by his illness. His decision to wear a suit that blended in with the light grey color of the set's backdrop. And, probably more damaging than these, the several on-camera shots of him wiping perspiration from his forehead while Kennedy was pressing him on the issues.

Jack Kennedy, by contrast, excelled in front of the camera. A polished public speaker, he appeared young, athletic, handsome, and poised. His practice of looking at the camera when answering questions—and not at the journalists who asked them, as Nixon did—made viewers see him as someone who was talking directly to them and who gave them straight answers.

When the debate ended, a large majority of television viewers recognized Kennedy as the winner. In contrast, most radio listeners thought that Nixon had won. Obviously, appearance and body language mattered!

Never again would political debates be the same. Today's candidates are fully aware of (and heavily coached on) the impact of appearance and nonverbal cues. Today's leaders should be just as aware.

Body Language at the Debates

During the presidential debates of 2008, I was asked by the State Department to post to its Web site my observations of the candidates' nonverbal behaviors. What struck me most strongly was that both candidates made "curb appeal" errors. In most of the debates, (then) Senator Obama minimized his emotional reactions and reinforced the impression that he was cerebral, remote, and "cold," and Senator McCain's forced grins and eye rolling in the third debate sent a negative signal that was reflected instantly in polls rating the candidates' likeability.

Warm and Authoritative Leaders

There are two sets of nonverbal signals that are especially important to the curb appeal of leaders. When first introduced to a leader, we immediately and unconsciously assess him or her for warmth and authority. Obviously the most appealing leaders are seen to encompass both qualities, and the least effective leaders are those we regard as cold and inept. But as Harvard Business School professor Teresa Amabile described in an aptly titled article, "Brilliant but Cruel," the problem is that we often see competence and warmth as being negatively related—warm leaders don't appear as intelligent or skilled as those who are more negative and meaner, and tough leaders are judged far less likeable.[5]

So the best leadership strategy is to embody both sets of traits—and to do so early and often. Let people see both sides of your leadership character. Let them know right from the beginning that you are caring and credible.

The Body Language of Warmth and Authority

Always remember that people will be watching your actions as a leader. The higher you go in the organization, the more people will be scrutinizing your behavior. If you want to be a great leader, you'll need to get used to people viewing and evaluating your every move. Many executives underestimate the importance of their behavior to the people they lead. But Sue, the savvy CEO of a telecommunications company, is not one of them. As Sue says, "I know that everything I do in the hallway is more important than anything I say in the meeting."

I've learned a lot about warmth by observing effective executives like Sue and noting how they work with their staffs. The best of these leaders connect with people in a way that makes them want to do a really good job because of that personal connection, affection, and respect. These "warm" leaders send signals of empathy, friendliness, and caring.

As a leader, you communicate warmth nonverbally with open body postures, palm-up hand gestures, a full-frontal body orientation, positive eye contact, synchronized movements, head nods, head tilts, and smiles. As you read the rest of this book (especially the chapters on negotiation, collaboration, and change management), you'll learn why these signals are so important—and when it's most effective to display them.

People also want leaders who display power, status, and confidence. Especially in times of chaos and confusion, employees look for leaders who project stability and certainty, who make them feel secure, and who they believe will achieve results. And they will assess you for these qualities through your nonverbal displays of authority.

As a leader, you show authority and power by your erect posture, command of physical space, purposeful stride (like that of Apple's CEO Steve Jobs as he moves across the stage during a presentation), and firm handshake, and through an array of hand signals including "steepling" and palm-down gestures that send nonverbal signals of authority. (Chapter Two will show you how to use these signals to your advantage in a business negotiation.)

What must be kept in mind, however, is that signals designed to project power and strength can be overdone or displayed inappropriately. For example, a nonverbal signal of confidence is to hold your head up—but if you tilt your head back even slightly, the signal changes to one of "looking down your nose." Similarly, a smile (which is the most positive and powerful display of warmth) can, as I'm sure you can imagine, work against you if you smile too much when delivering a serious message or stating an objection.

FIVE MISTAKES PEOPLE MAKE READING YOUR BODY LANGUAGE

The ability to instantly read body language is one of our basic survival instincts and can be traced back to primitive origins. But our ancient ancestors faced daily threats and challenges very different from those we confront in today's workplace. So, as innate as this ability may be, not all instant impressions are accurate. In fact, when people read your body language, you can count on them making these five major mistakes:

1. *They don't consider the context.* When it comes to body language, context is king. You can't make sense of someone's nonverbal message unless you understand the circumstances behind it. Context is a complex weave of variables including location, relationships, time of day, and past experience. Depending on the context, the same nonverbal signals can have totally different meanings. Take the simple shoulder shrug, for example: in a social setting, it can be a

sign of flirtation; when responding to a question, it becomes a nonverbal way to say "I don't know" or "I don't care"; it can be used by a coworker to minimize the importance of what you just said; and when accompanying a workplace directive, such as "Get the report to me by Monday," it serves to weaken the declaration.

Remember that your team members, colleagues, and staff can't possibly know all the variables that create the context of your actions. You yawn and stretch, and your staff assumes that you're bored—because no one realizes you've been up since dawn to place an overseas call. Or you hug a coworker and it looks like inappropriate behavior to passersby who don't know that her mother just died and you are comforting her.

2. *They find meaning in a single gesture.* As the gate-keepers, confidants, and (oftentimes) fierce protectors of the leaders they support, executive assistants are asked a lot of questions. But the question they hear most often is "What mood is the boss in?"

Of course! When you are a leader, people are on constant alert to find out if you are in a good mood (happy, positive, upbeat) or a bad mood (worried, angry, upset), because your mood is their "green light–red light" signal to approach or avoid. If you are in a good mood, it means there's an opportunity for people to bring up a concern, an idea, or a request. When you are in a bad mood, people will go out of their way to avoid dealing with you.

But even when people aren't inquiring directly about your state of mind, they will still be evaluating it through your body language. And this is where trouble can arise, because all too often they will be getting their information from a single nonverbal cue. And because the human brain pays more attention to negative messages than it does to positive ones, what people unconsciously look for and react to the most are signs that you are in a bad mood and not to be approached.

What this means in a business setting is that if you pass a colleague in the hallway and don't make eye contact, she may jump to the conclusion that you are upset with the report she just turned in. Or if you frown in a staff meeting, attendees may think you didn't like what you just heard—and they will keep their corroborating opinions to themselves. In fact, when you make any nonverbal display of anger, irritability, or annoyance, people are more likely to hold back their opinions, limit their comments, and look for ways to shorten their interaction with you.

3. *They don't know your baseline.* One of the keys to accurately reading body language is to compare someone's current nonverbal response to his or her baseline, or normal behavior. But if people haven't observed you over time, they have little basis for comparison. Here's an example from my previous book, *The Nonverbal Advantage*, that illustrates how easy it is to misinterpret nonverbal signals under these circumstances.[6]

I was giving a presentation to the CEO of a financial services company, outlining a speech I was scheduled to deliver to his leadership team the next day. And it wasn't going well.

Our meeting lasted almost an hour, and through that entire time, the CEO sat at the conference table with his arms tightly crossed. None of my efforts at small talk loosened him up. He didn't once smile or nod encouragement. So I launched directly into my remarks, and when I finished, he said thank you (without making eye contact) and left the room.

I assumed his nonverbal communication was telling me that my speaking engagement would be canceled (I'm an expert at this, after all). But when I walked to the elevator, the CEO's assistant came to tell me how impressed her boss had been with what I had to say. I was shocked, and asked how he would have reacted had he not liked it. "Oh," said the assistant, her smile acknowledging that she had previously seen that reaction as well. "He would have gotten up in the middle of your presentation and walked out!"

The only nonverbal signals that I had received from that CEO were ones I judged to be negative. What I didn't realize was that, for this individual, this was standard operating procedure.

4. *They evaluate through the filter of personal biases.* There is a woman in my yoga class who liked me from the moment we met. I'd prefer to believe that her positive response was a result of my charismatic body language, but I know for a fact that it's because I resemble her favorite aunt.

So sometimes biases work in your favor. The term "halo effect," coined by psychologist E. L. Thorndike, describes how our perception of one desirable trait in a person can cause us to judge that person more positively overall.[7] If we view someone as likeable, for instance, we often also perceive him or her as more honest and trustworthy as well.

I've noticed that it goes even further. Some leaders are so well liked that the people they lead forgive, overlook, or even deny negative characteristics—another example of the emotional brain overriding the analytic brain (but not so good for getting accurate performance feedback).

Biases can also work against you. What if, instead of a beloved aunt, I had reminded my yoga classmate of someone she despised? I might have overcome it with time, but you can bet that her initial response to me would have reflected that negative bias.

There is a test that's available on a Harvard University Web site—the Implicit Association Test (IAT)—that measures the extent to which individuals associate various characteristics, such as race, sexual preference, and weight, with positive or negative attributes. The test reveals that even when people consciously believe otherwise, they respond in ways that reveal their unconscious biases.[8]

5. *They evaluate through the filter of cultural biases.* When it comes to dealing with a multicultural workforce, we create all sorts of obstacles by failing to consider cultural biases—theirs and ours. And when it comes to

cross-cultural nonverbal communication, those biases can appear in all sorts of ways.

As a leader, you will be judged by behaviors that may include how close you stand to a colleague in conversation, how much or little you touch others, and the amount of eye contact you use (and expect in return) when meeting with a subordinate. Depending on the observer's cultural bias, your body language will be labeled "right" or "wrong."

WHEN YOUR BODY DOESN'T MATCH YOUR WORDS

The senior vice president who addressed the conference in New York made a basic body language blunder when his gesture didn't match his words. And it is this kind of misaligned signaling that people pick up on more quickly and critically than almost any other. In fact, their brains register the incongruence in ways that can be scientifically measured.

Neuroscientist Spencer D. Kelly of Colgate University studies the effects of gestures by using an electroencephalograph (EEG) machine to measure "event-related potentials"—brain waves that form peaks and valleys. One of these valleys, dubbed N400, occurs when subjects are shown gestures that contradict what's spoken. This is the same brain-wave pattern that occurs when people listen to nonsensical language. So, in a very real way, when your words say one thing and your gestures indicate another, you don't make sense.[9]

Sometimes a leader's incongruent body language is so obvious that it's almost comical. Here is an e-mail sent to me from a government committee member: "I was in a very serious meeting in Washington DC and the person making the presentation was telling the group how much he welcomed any input we could provide. At the same time he was using both his hands to nonverbally push the entire group away. The amazing thing was that he repeated this sequence several times, always saying that he would welcome our input while making exactly the same 'push back' gesture. It was all I could do not to absolutely lose it and laugh out loud. I almost did, but that would not have been good!"

But most often a leader's incongruence is no laughing matter. Here's an e-mail from an office worker in an insurance company: "My boss drives us crazy with her mixed messages. She says things like, 'You are always welcome in my office' and 'You are all an important part of the team.' At the same time, her nonverbal communication is constantly showing how unimportant we are to her. She never makes eye contact, will shuffle papers when others talk, writes e-mail while we answer her questions and generally does not give her full attention. In fact, we don't even rate her half attention! Then she wonders why her staff doesn't seek her out."

THE BODY LANGUAGE OF A GREAT LEADER

At some point in the coaching process, clients will usually ask (and you may be wondering too), "Does this mean I have to inhibit every spontaneous gesture and expression for fear of sending the wrong message?"

Well, yes!

Relax, I'm only joking. Successful leaders don't memorize "the right" physical gestures and facial expressions to display at appropriate times as though they were some kind of preprogrammed robot. (And, by the way, leaders who try to do this actually look like robots.) But they are aware that their body language dramatically impacts colleagues, clients, and staff. They understand that for a variety of reasons, even the most well-meaning behaviors will sometimes be misinterpreted, and they are ever alert to finding authentic ways to align their nonverbal communication with the messages they want to deliver.

The next three chapters will show you exactly how they do that.

2

NEGOTIATION

Reading and Using Body Language
to Your Advantage

A few years ago, a group of rising-star executives gathered at MIT to take part in a special competitive event. Each was to present a business plan to be evaluated by the entire group. The best ideas would then be recommended to a team of venture capitalists for final evaluation. Participants saw this as a great opportunity to see how their ideas compared to those of others in an elite peer group.

If you had been one of those chosen executives, how would you have prepared for the event? Would you have concentrated on formulating a coherent description of your business plan? Developed a strategy for convincing others? Practiced your presentation skills?

The leaders at the MIT event probably did all of these. But on the day of the competition, an additional component was added to the mix—one nobody had prepared for. Each presenter was outfitted with a specially designed digital sensor, worn like an ID badge. This device, called a Sociometer, would be taking notes on each presentation along with the rest of the group, but not on the merits of what was being said. Unbeknownst to the presenters, the Sociometer would be recording what *wasn't* being said: tonal variety, vocal nuance, physical activity, energy level, even the number of smiles and nods exchanged between presenter and audience.

MIT's Sociometer

At the end of the meeting, the group selected the ideas they agreed would sell best. And, with no knowledge of any actual content, the Sociometer readings also predicted (with nearly perfect accuracy) which business plans the presenters would choose. That's because, while the group thought they were making rational choices, the researchers at the MIT Media Lab, who had developed the digital device, knew better. What convinced the executive group is the same set of signals that also predict the outcome of any negotiation you may be involved in—your nonverbal signals and interactions.[1]

Every aspect of leadership requires some form of negotiation. Leaders negotiate salary and title before accepting a job offer; they negotiate deadlines for projects; they negotiate for funding, resources, and recognition for their departments or teams; and (depending on their specific role within the organization), they negotiate with an array of customers, clients, consultants, and suppliers. Increasingly in this interconnected business world, they also negotiate with competitors who have become allies in a current project.

Proficiency in negotiation takes good body language skills. Think of it this way: in any negotiation, you are communicating over two channels—verbal and nonverbal—resulting in two distinct conversations going on at the same time. Although a well-designed bargaining strategy is obviously important, it's not the most important message you send. Communication research shows that in a thirty-minute negotiation, two people can send over eight hundred different nonverbal signals.[2] If you focus on the verbal exchange alone and ignore the nonverbal element, you stand a high chance of coming away from that negotiation wondering why in the world your brilliantly constructed bargaining plan didn't work the way it was supposed to.

Savvy negotiators have learned how to read and use body language to their advantage. This chapter will help you become aware of how nonverbal messages are being delivered and interpreted in a negotiation. It will show you how to pay attention, identify a baseline, consider the context, and evaluate gesture clusters. You will learn to accurately read your counterparts' body language and to identify how your own gestures and expressions support or sabotage your bargaining position.

FOUR TIPS FOR READING BODY LANGUAGE

When people find out that I write and speak about body language, they immediately become nervous and self-conscious. They react as if I could detect their innermost thoughts and motives with a single glance.

Well, I can't.

Neither can you. But what you can do is realize that you are "reading" people all the time without knowing it—and are prone to making the same snap decisions about others that they are making about you. You can greatly improve your accuracy by bringing awareness into what has been a mostly subconscious process. Here are four tips to help you get started.

First Tip: Pay Attention

Many negotiators miss valuable opportunities to read their counterparts' body language simply because they don't pay attention. They make the mistake of looking down at the papers or contract presented instead of staying alert to nonverbal signals. So the next time your opponent presents a written document for you to read, resist the temptation to look at it. Instead, ask him to tell you what it says, and watch his body language as he does. You'll learn so much more.

Second Tip: Identify a Baseline

To accurately read body language, you first need to establish a person's normal—or baseline—behavior. If you don't take the time to do this, you are most likely going to misinterpret his or her signals. "Baselining" entails observing people when they are not stressed or pressured. It takes only a few minutes to get a feel for how someone acts in a relaxed or neutral setting, and the best time to do this is before the negotiation starts—for instance, while having coffee and making small talk. While you are chatting informally, do a quick "body scan" and notice the following:

- How animated is your counterpart? (Does he or she show you a mobile, expressive, apparently candid face, or are you looking at the unreadable poker face of a professional card player?)

- How much eye contact are you experiencing?

- How much smiling are you being shown? Does the smile seem natural and genuine, or forced and perhaps nervous or manipulative?

- How much hand gesturing is your counterpart using? Which gestures are you seeing most frequently?

- What sort of posture is being displayed: Erect? Slouched? Shoulders back or hunched? Head held high—thrust forward—turned aside?

- When your counterpart is seated at the conference table, what position does he or she take: Upright? Leaning back? Forward? Sideways or square to the table? Legs crossed, or feet flat on the floor? Hands folded or spread on the table? Resting on or holding the chair arms? Out of sight in the lap?

Once you've determined how your counterpart uses his or her body in a relaxed, informal context, you'll have a baseline against which to compare possibly meaningful body language deviations during the negotiation process itself. (Later in the course of the meeting, whenever you see deviations from baseline behavior, think about what just happened to prompt the change. Did you alter your body language? Did you ask a question or touch on a particular issue? Did someone else enter the room or join the conversation?) For now, all you are doing is looking to identify behaviors that are normal for that person.

Third Tip: Evaluate Gestural Clusters

Nonverbal cues occur in what is called a *gesture cluster*—a
group of movements, postures, and actions that reinforce a
common point. Trying to decipher body language from a
single gesture is like trying to find narrative meaning in a
single word. However, when words appear in sentences,
or gestures in clusters, their meaning becomes clearer.
For example, although a person's fidgeting may not mean
much by itself, if that person is also avoiding eye contact,
wringing his hands, and pointing his feet toward the door,
there's a very good chance that he's distressed and wants
to leave. A good rule is to look for three body language
signals that reinforce the same nonverbal message.

Fourth Tip: Consider the Context

In an audience, I expect people in the first row to be
sitting with their arms crossed. I know that without a
row of chairs in front of them, most people will create a
barricade with their arms (at least initially, before they
warm up to the speaker and lower their guard). Likewise,
if a person sits in a chair that doesn't have armrests, I
realize that the limited option increases the likelihood of
crossed arms—as would a drop in room temperature. And
if someone were deep in thought, pacing back and forth
with crossed arms, I'd know that this was a common way
to increase concentration and persistence. It's the same

arm gesture in all situations, but the meaning changes dramatically with the context.

When people are interacting, their gender and relationship determine much of the context. The same man talking with a female colleague, his boss, or a male subordinate may display very different body language with each. (And his baseline behavior for each relationship would also change accordingly.) Such variables as time of day, expectations based on past encounters, and whether the interaction is formal or informal also need to be taken into consideration when you evaluate meaning. Of course there will always be aspects of context you won't be aware of. An erect posture may signal a tough bargaining position, or it may simply indicate a stiff back.

ARE THEY WITH YOU OR AGAINST YOU?

In a negotiation, signs of engagement and disengagement are the most important ones to monitor in the other person's body language. Engagement behaviors indicate interest, receptivity, or agreement; disengagement behaviors signal that a person is bored, angry, or defensive. And because you'll be looking for gesture clusters, you'll need to know how to identify these signals from "top to bottom" in a variety of facial expressions, head movements, hand and arm gestures, torso positions, and leg and feet placements.

This may sound like an impossible task, especially because you'll be conducting a conversation at the same time, but remember that you've been reading body language your entire life. All that is different now is that you're taking this innate but unconscious skill into awareness—and by doing so, gaining insight, accuracy, and control.

The Power of Engagement

Over the years, I've noticed that parties are more likely to reach an agreement if they begin the negotiation displaying engaged body language. Interestingly, that positive result is the same whether the display was the product of an unconscious choice or a strategic decision.

The Eyes Have It

You present two written options, and you notice that the gaze of your counterpart lingers longer on one than on the other. If, in addition, you see his eyes open wide and his pupils dilate, you know for certain that he has a much greater interest in this option.

In general, people tend to look longer and with more frequency at people or objects they like. A person may be trying to look uninterested, but his eyes will keep returning to the object that attracts him.

The same is true with eye contact. Most of us are comfortable with eye contact lasting about three seconds, and a prolonged mutual gaze without breaking can make us nervous. But when we like or agree with someone, we automatically increase the amount of time we look into his or her eyes.

Disengagement triggers the opposite gaze reactions. The amount of eye contact decreases, as we tend to look away from things that distress us and people we don't like. Similarly, a counterpart who is bored or restless may avoid eye contact by gazing past you, defocusing, looking down, glancing around the room. or even closing eyes, effectively blocking you from view. And, instead of opening wide, eyes that signal disengagement will narrow slightly. In fact, eye squints can be observed as people read contracts or proposals, and when they occur, it is almost always a sign of having seen something troubling or problematic.

Researchers have known for years that eye pupil size is a major clue in determining a person's emotional responses. The pupils are a part of our body we have practically no control over. Therefore, pupil dilation can be a very effective way to gauge someone's interest. Pupils dilate for various reasons, including memory load and cognitive difficulty, but pupils also dilate when we have positive feelings about the person we're talking to or the object we're looking at. (And when someone is less than receptive, his or her pupils will automatically constrict.)

Normal pupil size and the dilated eyes of engagement

Another set of eye cues to monitor is conjugate lateral eye movements. These are the sudden and involuntary eye shifts to the left or right which indicate that the listener is actively processing what you just said. When you notice this happening, you can be assured that you have your counterpart's interest and attention.

The Look of Business

Imagine a triangle with the base at eye level and the peak at mid-forehead. That is the most appropriate gaze area when conducting business. When you invert that triangle and drop your gaze more to the mouth, which is more appropriate in a personal relationship, you send signals of flirting.

The Head, Face, and Neck

Typically, someone who is in agreement with you will smile and nod as you speak. Disagreement shows up in compressed or pursed lips, lowered eyebrows, a tense mouth, clenched jaw muscles, head shaking, or a head turned slightly away, so eye contact becomes sidelong.

The pursed lips of disengagement

I was once asked by an SVP of human resources to work with a leader whose micromanagement was limiting her team's effectiveness. When I met with the leader, Judith, she was effusive with her praise—going on and on about how much she had heard about me and how delighted she was to have me as her coach. However, I noticed that her smiles always seemed forced. I expected to discover that she wasn't as delighted with me as she claimed and that she was putting on a show for the HR executive's sake. I was right. As time went on, it became clear that Judith had no interest in working with me (or any other coach) and no intention of changing her management style.

Smiles are often used as a polite response and to cover up other emotions, but these faked smiles involve the mouth only. Unless someone is expressing genuine pleasure or happiness, it's hard to produce a real smile—the kind that crinkles the corners of the eyes and lights up the entire face.

There are other ways that real emotions emerge, regardless of the effort to suppress them. A jump of the Adam's apple is one of these—an unconscious sign of emotional anxiety, embarrassment, or stress. You may notice this upward and downward neck movement when your male counterpart (men have a larger mass of cartilage that makes up the laryngeal prominence—Adam's apple) hears something he strongly dislikes or disagrees with.

Hands and Arms

In general, the more open the position of your counterpart's arms, the more receptive he or she will be to the negotiation process. Watch for expansive, welcoming gestures that seem to flow naturally from a person's behavior. When someone reaches toward you or uses a lot of open-hand gestures, it is usually a positive signal of interest and receptivity.

By contrast, people who are defensive or angry may protectively fold their arms across their chest, clench their hands into fists, or tightly grip their arm or wrist. Boredom is often indicated by doodling in a way that seems to absorb the doodler's complete attention, drumming fingers on the table, or using a hand to support the head. Brushing a hand across the knee or thigh, as if dusting away invisible crumbs, is a sign of being dismissive.

As the negotiation progresses, hand and arm movements are one of the best indicators of changes in the emotions of the participants. For example, when you start the negotiation, your counterpart's hands may be resting openly on the table. If they pull away or withdraw to under the table, it's probably a signal that something unsettling or unwanted just happened. And if negotiators are about to make a sincere disclosure, they will usually place both hands on the table and gesture as they speak.

Shoulders and Torso

The shoulders and torso play an important role in nonverbal communication. The more your counterparts like and agree with you, the more they will lean toward you and the more closely they will stand before or beside you. In contrast, when you say or do things your counterparts disagree with or are uncertain about, the more they will tend to lean back and create more space between you. And watch for shrugging shoulders that signal rejection in response to an idea you've just proposed.

When you see people turn their shoulders and torso away from you, you've probably lost their interest. In fact, orienting away from someone in this manner almost always conveys detachment or disengagement, regardless of the words spoken. When people are engaged, they will face you directly, "pointing" at you with their torso. However, the instant they feel uncomfortable, they will turn away—giving you "the cold shoulder." In a negotiation, this torso shifting can occur at any time. Distressful news one minute and favorable news the next will be reflected by a torso shift toward you or away, depending on how someone feels about what was just said. And if someone is feeling defensive, you may see an attempt to shield the torso with a purse, briefcase, laptop, and so on.

People who are in agreement tend to mirror one another's behavior. One will lead and the other will follow. If you notice that your fellow negotiator has assumed the same basic body orientation as yours, move slightly and see if she follows suit. If she does, you know you've made a positive connection.

What Feet Can Tell You

At a recent conference where I was a speaker, I arrived a day early to view other presenters and to get acquainted with the audience. One of the sessions I saw was an interview with the president of a financial institution. The interviewer and interviewee were seated onstage in chairs facing the audience.

From a body language perspective, it was fascinating. At first, the executive's entire body signaled both warmth and authority as he shared his philosophy of "relationship banking" and the importance of employees to his company's brand. Then came a series of questions about executive compensation. As the bank president responded to these inquiries, his expressions and gestures stayed constant—but his "foot language" changed dramatically: from a comfortable, loose leg cross, the executive suddenly locked his ankles tightly together, pulled them back under his chair, and began to make tiny kicks with both feet. He then recrossed his ankles and kicked his feet again. This behavior continued throughout the entire set of compensation questions.

Was the executive comfortable addressing this issue? Well, his upper body would have you believe he was. And if that were all you could see (if, for instance, he had been sitting behind a desk or standing behind a lectern), you might have been convinced he was at ease. But his feet told an entirely different story—one of stress and anxiety.

Our feet and legs are not only our primary means of locomotion but also in the forefront of "fight, flight, or freeze" reactions. And they are "programmed" to respond faster than the speed of thought. Before we've had time to develop any conscious plan, our limbic brain has already made sure that, depending on the situation, our feet and legs are geared to freeze in place, run away, or kick out in defense.

When people try to control their body language, they focus primarily on facial expressions and hand and arm gestures. That leaves their feet and legs "unrehearsed." I advise my clients to "accidentally" drop a pen during a negotiation so that they can look under the conference table and check out foot and leg positions. If someone is sitting with ankles crossed and legs stretched forward, they are probably feeling positively toward you. But when you see feet pulled away from you, wrapped in a tight ankle lock, pointed at the exit, or wrapped around the legs of a chair, you would be wise to suspect withdrawal and disengagement.

See what their feet are telling you.

The following are other signals from feet:

- High-energy heel bouncing almost always indicates that the party involved has "happy feet"—and is feeling pretty good about his bargaining position. And if your seated opponent rocks back on her heels and raises her toes, she probably thinks she has the upper hand.

- Bouncing legs that suddenly go still are probably a sign of heightened anticipation—the equivalent of holding your breath.

- Crossed legs send their own set of cues. If the foot on the leg that is crossed on top is pointing toward you, the person is most likely engaged. If the opposite leg is crossed so that the top foot is pointing away, the person may be withdrawing.

Beware of Crossed Legs

Crossed legs can have a devastating effect on a negotiation. In *How to Read a Person Like a Book*, authors Gerard I. Nierenberg and Henry H. Calero reported that the number of times settlements were reached increased greatly when both negotiators had uncrossed their legs. In fact, they found that out of two thousand videotaped transactions, not one resulted in a settlement when even one of the negotiators had his or her legs crossed.[3]

DEALING WITH THE DISENGAGED

When you notice your counterpart exhibiting any of the disengagement signals, there are six things you can do in response:

1. Check your body position. Are you exhibiting any closed or disengaged behaviors that your counterpart may be mimicking or reacting to? If so, change your body language to signal more openness and warmth.

2. Do nothing now, but recognize that you have hit someone's "hot button"—and use this insight as you continue to negotiate.

3. Make the person move. For example, if your counterpart's arms and legs are crossed, lean forward and hand him or her something—a brochure, a contract, or a cup of coffee.

4. Change your "pitch." Realize that what you are proposing isn't being well received, and now may be the time for "Plan B."

5. Bring the person's disengagement behavior to his or her attention. The response to someone's continual fidgeting, lack of eye contact, and so on might be, "It looks as if this may be a bad time for us to talk. Would you prefer to postpone this meeting until tomorrow?"

6. Watch for signals that indicate a positive change. Many men who have their arms crossed in a defensive

53

gesture will also have their jackets buttoned. Someone who has just favorably changed his mind might uncross his arms and instinctively unbutton his jacket.

ARE THEY BLUFFING?

Wouldn't it be great to know when someone is bluffing? And wouldn't it be nice if exposing falsehoods were as easy as it appears to be on television shows like *Lie to Me* and *The Mentalist?* But of course deception detection is more complex than that. What are often mistaken for signs of lying are actually self-pacifying gestures that everyone uses to relieve stress.

The newest technology in the field of lie detection is the use of fMRIs to track brain activity as a lie is formed. Basically, what researchers are finding is that fibbing requires more cognitive resources than being truthful. One theory, posed by Daniel Langleben, a psychiatrist and neuroscientist at the University of Pennsylvania, is that in order to tell a lie, the brain first has to stop itself from telling the truth, then create the deception, monitor to keep future statements aligned with the lie, and deal with the accompanying emotions of guilt and anxiety—this process is what the fMRIs are charting.[4]

But if you don't have access to an fMRI machine, how can you tell when someone is bluffing? Well, it's extremely difficult if you're dealing with a very clever liar or a superb actor. But for the vast majority of the individuals you negotiate with, the act of lying triggers a heightened stress response. And these signs are obvious, if you know where to look.

To increase your chances of spotting a bluff, watch for the following body language cues:

- *Increased blink rate.* Increased blinking is associated with stress and other negative emotions. So when most people are bluffing, their blink rate increases dramatically. Police interrogators and customs inspectors look for a change in the blink rate that might signify areas where the person is trying to cover something up.

- *Pupil dilation.* Although dilation can be triggered when we look at someone or something we are interested in, it also frequently occurs when a lie is being told. In this case, the dilation is attributed to a liar's increased tension and concentration.

- *Prolonged eye contact.* One body language myth to be aware of is that all bluffers will avoid looking into your eyes. Although some liars avoid or decrease eye contact, this behavior is widely known and fairly easy to control. In fact, many liars will overcompensate with too much eye contact.

- *Foot movements.* When trying to deceive, people will often display nervousness and anxiety through increased foot movements. Feet may fidget, shuffle, and wind around each other or around the furniture. They might stretch and curl to relieve tension, or even kick out in a sublimated flight gesture.

- *Face touching.* A person's nose may not grow when he tells a lie, but watch closely and you'll notice that when someone is about to lie or make an outrageous statement, he'll often unconsciously rub his nose. (This is most likely because a rush of adrenaline opens the capillaries and makes his nose itch.) Mouth touching is another gesture commonly seen in people who are feeling doubtful or being untruthful.

- *Response time.* When the falsehood is planned (and rehearsed), deceivers start their answers more quickly than truth-tellers. If taken by surprise, however, the liar takes longer to respond—as the process of inhibiting the truth and creating a lie takes extra time. That's why police interrogators tell me that the most common vocal deception clues are pauses that are too long or too frequent. Hesitating when responding to a question or responses that are filled with several short pauses nearly always arouse their suspicion.

- *Hidden hands.* Whereas open-palm gestures indicate candor, hidden hands (hands kept under the table or in pockets) may be a signal that someone has something to hide or is reluctant to participate in the conversation.

- *Arrested gestures.* Familiar hand, shoulder, and head gestures that seem unnaturally to be arrested midperformance can often indicate an attempt to deceive. A shrug that stops midway, a one-shoulder shrug, an incomplete hand gesture, a nod or cock of the head that seems to stop short—any of these, typically, can signal an attempt to suppress or alter information.

- *Lack of nonverbal signals.* When bluffing, people tend to reduce all nonverbal displays in the hope that their bodies won't "leak" the truth and expose the bluff. So be aware of the high-energy negotiator who suddenly gets much less expressive.

BODY LANGUAGE GUIDELINES FOR NEGOTIATORS

Nonverbal communication works both ways. If your counterpart is an experienced negotiator, chances are that he or she will be observing and assessing your body language from the minute you walk into the meeting room. Here are five body language guidelines to help you hold your own in the body language arena.

1. People form an opinion of you within the first seven seconds. Be aware of this and use it to your advantage.

It all begins with the right attitude. Regardless of how tiring or frustrating your day may have been, before you enter the negotiation room, pull your shoulders back, hold your head high, take a deep breath, and walk in as your "best self"—exuding ease and energy.

Just after entering the meeting room, stop for a moment and look around at the person or group that has already assembled. Open your eyes slightly larger than usual. This will trigger an "eyebrow flash" (a slight upward movement that is a universal signal of recognition and welcome). Smile.

Make eye contact with all your counterparts. A simple way to enhance positive eye contact is to make a mental note of the eye color of everyone you meet. You don't have to remember the color; just gaze long enough to notice it. With this one exercise, you will dramatically increase your likeability factor.

2. Initiate a great handshake.

The handshake—it's the most familiar and traditional of nonverbal business greetings, but hidden within such a seemingly simple formality is an opportunity to make a lasting impression. You can develop an immediate and positive connection with someone from the touching of hands.

Let's shake on it!

- Whenever possible, you should initiate the handshake. Lean forward and extend your hand with your palm facing sideways.
- Keep your body squared off to the other person—facing him or her fully.
- Maintain eye contact and continue to smile.
- Make sure you have palm-to-palm contact and that the web of your hand (the skin between your thumb and first finger) touches the web of the other person's.
- Press firmly—people will judge you as indecisive or weak if you offer a limp grip—but don't be overly aggressive and squeeze too hard.
- Hold the other person's hand a second longer than you are naturally inclined to do. This conveys additional sincerity and quite literally "holds" the other person's attention while you exchange greetings.
- Start talking before you let go: "It's great to see you" or "I'm so glad to be here." If you are meeting for the first time, introduce yourself.
- When you break eye contact, don't look down (it's a submission signal). Rather, keep your head up and move your eyes to the side.

3. Continue building rapport.

In negotiations, rapport is the foundation for a win-win outcome. Everything you have done from the time you entered the room until now has been geared to send rapport-building nonverbal statements. To continue building rapport, remember to maintain positive eye contact, lean forward, use head nods of encouragement, and smile when appropriate.

The most powerful sign of rapport—and one that you already do (unconsciously) around people you like and respect—is to mirror the other person's body postures, gestures, expressions, breathing pattern, and so on. Mirroring builds agreement, but if you use mirroring as a technique, be subtle. Allow two or three seconds to go by before gradually changing your body language to (more or less) reflect that of the other person.

Mirroring signals liking and interest.

One executive told me that in a negotiation session, he often mirrors the person he's dealing with in order to get a better sense of what he or she is experiencing. I've noticed this as well. Our bodies and emotions are so closely linked that by assuming another person's posture, you are not only gaining rapport but actually "getting a feel" for his or her frame of mind.

Try this: when seated at a conference table across from your counterpart, push back from the table and lean away from him or her. Most probably the other negotiator will react in kind, and he or she will back away from you. (When this happens, see if the tone of the conversation also shifts to reflect the disengagement.) Now lean forward and put your hands on the table, look him or her in the eyes, and smile. Watch as the interaction warms up and is much more friendly and open. That's how fast you can build or break rapport.

4. Display confidence.

One Saturday morning a couple of years ago, I spoke at Book Passage in Corte Madera, California—a wonderful and rare example of a thriving independent bookstore. Sitting in the front row of the audience was a young woman who had seen me on a local television show and had been practicing body language to improve her confidence. She told the audience how my tips helped her buy a new car: "There I was, facing the salesman, using a 'high-confidence' hand gesture [the steeple position in which the palms separate slightly, fingers of both hands spread, and fingertips touch] as I stated what I wanted in the deal. The salesman countered with an arrogant body posture in which he put both hands behind his head, crossed his legs, and leaned way back. But I didn't let it faze me. I kept 'the steeple' pointed right at him and stuck to my guns. And, guess what—I got everything I asked for!"

You've probably seen the steeple gesture. It's a favorite of executives, physicians, lawyers, and politicians, and it conveys a sense of superiority about the issue being discussed. So if you employ that gesture, use it sparingly, and only at those moments when you need to emphasize a point. (Speakers who overuse the steeple gesture look stagey and insincere.)

Steepling signals confidence and certainty.

People automatically pronate their hands (rotate their palms down) when they feel strongly about something. In essence, gestures with palms exposed show a willingness to negotiate on a particular point, and palms down indicate that you are closed to negotiation. In fact, a definitive gesture of authority when you speak is to place both hands, palms down, on the table.

I'm not saying that a single gesture will get you everything you're after, but I can assure you that during any negotiation, projecting confidence is crucial. If your body language suggests that you are tentative or unsure, your counterpart may assume that you are not assertive enough to maintain your negotiation position.

There are many nonverbal signals of confidence: showing your torso is one way of demonstrating a high level of confidence, security, or trust. The more you cover your torso with folded arms, crossed legs, and so on, the more it appears that you need to protect or defend yourself. Feet also say a lot about your self-confidence. When you stand with your feet close together, you can seem timid or hesitant. But when you widen your stance, relax your knees, and center your weight in your lower body, you look more "solid" and sure of yourself.

When you need to be seen as assertive, remember that power is displayed by height and space. If you stand, you will look more powerful to those who are seated, especially if you stand with your hands on your hips. If you move around, the additional space you take up adds to that impression. If you are sitting, you can still project power by stretching your legs and arms and by spreading out your belongings on the conference table and claiming more territory. Another dominance display is to lean back with your hands behind your head and your legs in a wide-four cross. (The position that the car salesman took.) I rarely advise men to take this position—and women never cross their legs like this—because it often conveys arrogance instead of confidence.

Congruent hand gestures that supplement the points you're making can convey energy, excitement, and passion. But overgesturing with flailing arms (especially when hands are raised above the shoulders) can make you appear out of control, less believable, and less powerful.

5. Defuse a strong argument with alignment.

Often strong verbal argument comes from a negotiator's need to be heard and acknowledged. If you physically align yourself with that person (sitting or standing shoulder to shoulder facing the same direction), you will defuse the situation. And, by the way, a move that will escalate the argument is to square your body to the other person or to move in closer.

6. Make a positive final impression.

In the same way you conveyed energy and ease during your entrance and projected confidence throughout the negotiation process, be sure you also make a strong exit. Stand tall, shake hands warmly, and leave your counterpart with the impression that you are someone he or she should look forward to dealing with in the future.

■ ■

In a high-stakes negotiation, as well as in everyday bargaining situations, body language skills can give you an advantage. With practice, you will be able to spot deception, to know when you have real agreement or a potential conflict, and, most of all, to feel more confident in your ability to present your thoughts and opinions with the clarity of purpose that comes only when your words and your body are saying the same thing.

3

LEADING CHANGE

The Nonverbal Key to Effective Change Management

L ast year I consulted with a company in the midst of major reorganization. I was hired to work with the executive team as they designed the change strategy and discussed ways to build employee engagement for the coming changes. At one of these planning sessions, a senior executive concurred that the restructuring would streamline and improve processes in her department. She seemed straightforward and fully supportive of the proposed changes. But at some point while I listened to her comments, it suddenly hit me: she didn't believe what she was saying. It was a combination of small things: her gestures came a beat too late, she made only minimal eye contact with the rest of the team, and her energy level was too low for someone who was supposed to be an enthusiastic supporter. She had done her best to be a good corporate soldier, but her body language revealed her true feelings. She didn't approve of the direction the company was taking.

I waited to see what would happen. Sure enough, a few weeks later, the executive resigned.

There is nothing that can invigorate a business like a major change. Maybe it's the adoption of a new strategic direction or the rollout of a new product line or the chance to acquire a competitor. But when leaders rally their troops to forge ahead, they often find they are leading a charge that employees (and even some other leaders) are unwilling or unready to embrace.

This chapter will show you how the brain is wired to reject change, and how emotions (yours and other people's) impact and influence an organization's ability to embrace change and transformation. And because most of the emotional content of a message is communicated nonverbally, you'll understand why body language expertise is crucial for anyone leading change. You'll learn to read the nonverbal signals of stress and resistance, how to use body language to be an effective speaker, and even how to "fake" charisma.

THIS IS YOUR BRAIN ON CHANGE

Don't you just hate dealing with people who fight against every plan for organizational change? You know the type: they're disruptive, set in their ways, and highly resistant to change, even when it is obviously in the best interest of the business. Well, guess what? New research suggests that those troublemaking, inflexible change resistors are ... all of us!

Recent advances in brain analysis technology allow researchers to track the energy of a thought moving through the brain in much the same way as they track blood flowing through the body. And as scientists watch different areas of the brain light up in response to specific thoughts, it becomes clear that we all react pretty much the same way to change: we try to avoid it.

Most of our daily activities, including many of our work habits, are repetitive tasks that take very little mental energy to perform. That's why "the way we've always done it" is so seductive. It not only seems right—it feels good. So it's no wonder that logic and common sense aren't enough to get people to sign up for the next corporate restructuring.

The Power of Emotion

Daniel Goleman's book *The New Leaders* starts with this statement: "Great leaders move us. They ignite our passion and inspire the best in us. When we try to explain why they are so effective, we speak of strategy, vision, or powerful ideas. But the reality is much more primal. Great leadership works through the emotions."[1]

I once asked the CEO of a technology company how his employees were dealing with a proposed change.

"We've presented all the facts," he replied. "But it would be much easier if people weren't so emotional!" In that organization, it seemed, employees were expected to analyze change and react rationally. Emotions were not supposed to be part of the equation.

It's an approach I've seen before: leaders quantifying everything they could to help employees reach objective conclusions. But, according to the neurologist and author Antonio Damasio, the center of our conscious thought (the prefrontal cortex) is so tightly connected to the emotion-generating amygdala that no one makes decisions based on pure logic. Damasio's research makes it clear that unconscious mental processes drive our decision making, and logical reasoning is really no more than a way to justify emotional choices.[2] The more I study organizational transformation, the more I find evidence that emotion, not logic, is at the heart of successful change.

Ever wonder why it's so hard to promote a new change initiative when past changes have failed? The answer demonstrates the power of emotion over logic. When people are in a situation that requires them to make a decision, their brain searches for past situations that seem similar to the current one in order to access the emotions that are attached to them. In the case of a failed change, the negative emotion gets immediately accessed and transferred to the new initiative—regardless of the rationale for or validity of the current change.

Motivating Change

Leaders use two sets of emotions to motivate change: negative and positive. In "crisis motivation" and "burning platform" rationales, the basic idea is to frighten employees into accepting change. And there is no doubt that negative emotions can be effective. Fear, anger, and disgust all trigger physiological responses that prepare the body for quick and specific actions.

But far more frequently, organizational change is neither quick nor specific. Rather, it is continuous, evolutionary, and often strangely ambiguous in nature, which means that managing such change requires much more innovative and flexible approaches. For this kind of change, negative emotions aren't much help at all. In fact, negativity significantly diminishes problem-solving abilities and narrows rather than expands creative thinking. That's why today's most effective change agents focus primarily on positive emotions that motivate people to commit to change and to act on that commitment.

Emotional Contagion

A business simulation experiment at Yale University gave two groups of people the assignment of deciding how much of a bonus to give each employee from a set fund of money. Each person in the group was to get as large a bonus as possible for certain employees, while being fair to the entire employee population. In one group, the

conflicting agendas led to stress and tension, whereas
in the second group, everyone ended up feeling good
about the result. The difference in emotional response was
created by the "plants"—actors who had been secretly
assigned to manipulate people's feelings about the project.
In the first group, the actor was negative and downbeat; in
the second, positive and upbeat. The emotional tone
of the meetings followed the lead of each actor—although
none of the group members understood how or why those
particular feelings had emerged.[3]

Emotional contagion is primarily a nonverbal process.
When one team member is angry or depressed, negative
body language can spread like a virus to the rest of the
team, affecting attitudes and lowering energy. Conversely,
happy and buoyant people are likely to make the entire
team feel upbeat and energized. Reviewing research on the
emotional contagion phenomenon, neurologist Richard
Restak concluded, "Emotions are infectious ... you can
catch the mood of other people just by sitting in the same
room with them."[4]

It's also true that emotional leads tend to flow from
the most powerful person in a group to the others.
During a major change, people will be on high alert,
constantly looking to their leader for emotional cues. If
you stay relaxed and optimistic, members of your work
groups will be more positive and more productive. If you
become upset, depressed, or angry, those emotions will
be "caught" by your team and expressed in a variety of

less-than-optimal results, including higher absenteeism and lower productivity.

THE BODY-MIND CONNECTION

As you know, when you're happy, you smile. But did you know that when you smile, you feel happier? Called "facial feedback," the effect is so powerful that even when you artificially produce a smile, the feedback from that facial expression affects your emotions and behavior. In one research project, participants were either prevented from smiling or encouraged to smile by holding a pencil in their mouths. Those who held a pencil in their teeth and thus were "forced" to smile rated cartoons as funnier than did those who held the pencil in their lips and could not smile.[5]

In another study, the University of California School of Medicine found that simply moving the facial muscles in the direction of fear, anger, disgust, sadness, happiness, and so on caused autonomic nervous system reactors—heart rate, blood pressure, skin temperature—to move in the direction of the respective emotion.[6]

And it isn't just facial expressions that have an impact on your nervous system and emotions. Your physical postures and movements are also involved. Take, for example, research at Radboud University, the Netherlands, that showed how backward motion was a powerful way to enhance cognitive control. The researchers found that when people encounter a difficult situation, getting them to step back (literally) boosted their ability to cope.[7]

Can You Fake Charisma?

Charisma has been described as personal magnetism or charm. Charismatic people are more outgoing, but they also spend more face-to-face time with others—picking up cues and drawing people out. It's not just what these leaders project that makes them charismatic; it's how they make others feel about themselves. Good leaders make employees believe in them. Great leaders make employees believe in themselves. It's all about dealing compassionately and effectively with people: listening, empathizing, and encouraging others to achieve outstanding results. So learning to read and respond to body language signals is crucial to leadership charisma.

But, of course, charisma is also about an individual's infectious positive attitude, personal energy, and enthusiasm, as projected through his or her body language. Nonverbal gestures are the most charismatic when they are organic and not affected, when they naturally enhance the verbal message. And as an executive coach, I help clients develop this aspect of charisma by teaching them to align their verbal (logical) and nonverbal (emotional) communication so closely that they are perceived as more poised, persuasive, and influential.

I also help them fake it.

Faking charisma takes a little practice—because, again, you're dealing with emotions. Trying to display confidence when you're actually feeling uncertain, or to be seen as upbeat and positive when (for any reason) you are feeling the opposite, is a tricky thing. But there are two valid options that will work: you can use a Method acting technique (I elaborate on this further in the next section), or you can work at the somatic level by understanding the body-mind connection.

According to research from Harvard Business School, subjects who held their bodies in certain physical poses changed their neuroendocrine levels, their emotions, and their behavior.[8] Here are findings from the study:

- Subjects holding their bodies in expansive, "high-power" poses (putting their hands behind their heads and their feet on the desk, or leaning over a desk and planting their hands far apart) for as little as two minutes stimulated higher levels of testosterone (the hormone linked to power and dominance) and lower levels of the stress hormone cortisol.

- In addition to causing hormonal shifts, power poses led to increased feelings of power and a greater tolerance for risk.

- People often are more influenced by how they feel about you than by what you're saying.

Learning body language skills isn't just helpful for communicating effectively to an audience; it also trains you to adopt positive, powerful, and uplifting postures and movements that in turn affect your mental state. As you assume the posture, gestures, expressions, and stance of confidence and charisma, you actually become more charismatic.

Emotional Memory—"the Method"

During the late 1800s, a new approach to acting was developed by a Russian actor, director, and coach, Constantin Stanislavsky. Called Method acting (or more simply, the Method), it was adopted by a new school of realistic actors including Marlon Brando, Al Pacino, and Robert DeNiro. The Method held that an actor's main responsibility was to be believed; and to reach this level of "believable truth," Stanislavsky employed methods such as "emotional memory," which drew on real but past emotions. For example, to prepare for a role that involves fear, an actor would remember something that had frightened him or her in the past, and bring that memory into the current role to make it emotionally valid.

As a leader, you will have different goals than an actor in a play, but the sense of conviction and believability you want to project will be fundamentally the same. For example, if you were going to announce an organizational change at an upcoming meeting and you wanted to exude confidence, here is how you'd go about it:

1. Think of an occasion when you were enthused, confident, and absolutely certain about a course of action. (This doesn't have to be taken from your professional life. What's important is identifying the right set of emotions.)

2. Picture that past event clearly in your mind. Recall the feeling of certainty, of enthusiasm, of clarity of purpose—and remember or imagine how you looked and sounded as you embodied that state of mind.

3. Picture yourself at the upcoming meeting with the same positive attitude and sense of confidence that you had in the past. The more you repeat this mental rehearsal—seeing yourself at the upcoming meeting assured, confident, and certain—the more you increase your ability to make the change announcement with body language that is triggered by that authentic, positive emotion.

Is Acting in Your Blood?

Nicholas Hall, a psychoneuroimmunologist and researcher, studied professional actors who portrayed contrasting personality types in a one-act play. He took blood samples before and after each performance and found that people who had been working with happy and uplifting scripts all day had healthy immune systems. Those people who had been working with depressing scripts all day showed a marked decrease in immune responsiveness.[9]

But whatever you do, don't try to simply suppress an emotion and think you are fooling anyone. Trying to suppress genuine emotions requires a great deal of conscious effort and is rarely successful. Whenever you try to conceal any strong feeling, your body "leaks" nonverbal cues that are picked up consciously or subconsciously by your audience.

The Problem with Suppression

Stanford University's research on emotional suppression shows why it's so difficult to hide our true feelings: the effort required takes a physical and psychological toll. Subjects instructed to conceal their emotions reported feeling ill at ease, distracted, and preoccupied. This was validated by a steady rise in their blood pressure. But another quite unexpected and, for our purposes, much more important finding showed a corresponding blood pressure rise in those listening to the subjects. The tension of suppression wasn't just palpable; it was contagious.[10]

ANNOUNCING CHANGE

The higher you advance in an organization, the more frequently you will be expected to give formal presentations. And nowhere will your speech-making talents be put more rigorously to the test then when you are announcing a major change.

Because of the personal and emotional nature of change, the audience will be monitoring your every move, and their brains are primed by evolution to look first for possible threats. A little nervousness at the beginning of the presentation will not be overlooked. Instead, it will be magnified and (most likely) interpreted negatively.

My best advice is never to promote a change you don't believe in—and always be as transparent and candid as possible. Doing so will help your body align authentically to reflect that openness. Even then you will need to pay close attention to your nonverbal signals. If you slouch, look down, clasp your hands in front of you, sway back and forth, or sound tentative, these behaviors (even if they are only nervous habits) can come across as uncertainty—or worse.

Body Language Onstage

Coaching executives in presentation skills, I know the importance of a well-written speech with an inspiring vision, engaging stories, self-deprecating humor, and personalized examples. But I also know that leaders can sabotage a great speech if they underestimate or ignore the power of body language.

I don't want you to make that mistake. Here are eight of the most important elements of body language onstage.

1. *Manage Your Stress Level* While you are waiting backstage, notice the tension in your body. Realize that some nervous energy is a good thing—it's what makes your presentation lively and interesting—but too much stress results in nonverbal behaviors that work against you.

Before you go onstage, stand or sit with your weight "centered"—evenly distributed on both feet or your "sit bones." Look straight ahead with your chin level to the floor and relax your throat. Take several deep "belly" breaths. Count slowly to six as you inhale and increase the tension in your body by making fists and tensing the muscles in your arms, torso, and legs. As you exhale, allow your hands, arms, and body to release and relax. Further loosen up by gently shaking one arm and then the other, and let your voice relax into its optimal pitch (a technique I learned from a speech therapist) by keeping your lips together and making the sounds "um hum, um hum, um hum."

2. *Focus on Your Message—All of It* Successful change communication involves several levels of information: the audience needs to understand the rationale for change (the marketplace realities that are behind the reason for change); they need to agree with the urgency for change (the conditions, challenges, and opportunities that make it imperative that the change happen now); and they need to believe they have the skills (or access to the skills) that are necessary to achieve the change. But you've seen why those factual components alone are not enough to compel people to action.

In order for people to be motivated to act, they need to be emotionally involved. So before you go onstage to deliver your message, concentrate on emotions and feelings. How do you personally emotionally connect with the proposed change? What do you feel about it? How do you want the audience to feel? What do you need to do nonverbally to embody those feelings?

3. Make a Confident Entrance Staying relaxed, walk out onstage with good posture, head held high, and a steady, smooth gait. When you arrive at center stage, stop, smile, raise your eyebrows, and slightly widen your eyes while you look around the room. A relaxed, open face and body tell your audience that you're confident and comfortable with the information you're delivering. Because audience members will be mirroring any tension you display, your state of comfort will also relax and reassure them. (This may sound like common sense, but I once worked with a manager who walked onstage with hunched shoulders, a furrowed brow, and squinted eyes. I watched the audience squirm in response. It was an unsettling way to begin a "Let's get together and support this change" speech.)

4. Maintain Eye Contact   Maintain steady eye contact with the audience throughout the talk. If you don't, you will quickly signal that you don't want to be there, that you aren't really committed to your message, or that you have something to hide.

Although it is physically impossible to maintain eye contact with the entire audience all the time, you can look at specific individuals or small groups, hold their attention briefly, and then move to another group or individual in another part of the room.

5. Ditch the Lectern   Get out from behind the lectern. A lectern not only covers up the majority of your body but also acts as a barrier between you and the audience. Practice the presentation so well that you don't need to read from a script. If you use notes, request a video prompter (or two) at the foot of the stage.

6. Talk with Your Hands   Speakers use hand gestures to underscore what's important and to express feelings, needs, and convictions. When people are passionate about what they are saying, their gestures become more animated. That's why gestures are so critical and why getting them right in a presentation connects so powerfully with an audience. If you don't use them (if you let your hands hang limply to your sides or you clasp them in the classic "fig leaf" position), it suggests that you don't recognize the crucial issues, have no emotional investment in the issues, or are an ineffective communicator.

There are three categories of gestures—emblems, pacifiers, and illustrators. Emblematic gestures have an agreed-on meaning to a group and can be understood without words. (The finger-to-lips "be quiet" gesture is one example.) Pacifiers are gestures that people use to relieve stress. (More about these later in the chapter.) Illustrative hand gestures develop simultaneously with speech. They are so tightly linked with speech that we rarely communicate without them. Illustrators help us find the right words and make the expression of thoughts more emphatic and precise. Even blind people use illustrators when speaking—just as all of us gesture when talking on the telephone.

Authentic illustrators occur split seconds before the words that accompany them. They either will precede the word or will be coincident with the word, but will never come after the word. (This is one reason why trying to choreograph gestures in advance when preparing a presentation seldom works. The timing is off.)

If I were working with you before an important presentation, my advice would be to focus on the importance of your message and the emotions behind it, and let your natural ability to illustrate take over automatically as you speak—just as it does when you are chatting with friends.

But if you feel that your gestures do need a bit of rehearsing, let me remind you of a few basic guidelines:

- Palms facing straight up communicate the lack of something that the speaker needs or is requesting.

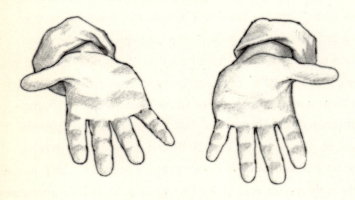

He needs something.

- Gestures with palms showing (tilted to a forty-five-degree angle) signal candor and openness.

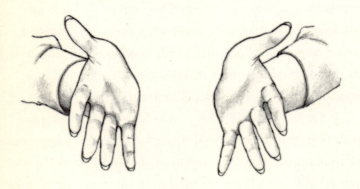

She's open and candid.

- Palm-down gestures signal power and certainty.

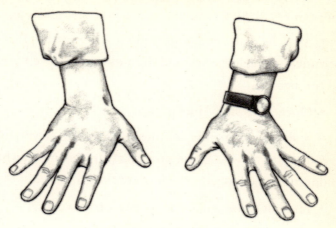

He's made up his mind.

- Vertical palm gestures with a rigid hand are often used to beat out a rhythm that gives emphasis to certain words.

She's adding emphasis.

- Steepling signals confidence and expertise about the point you are making.

- Arms held at waist height, and gestures within that horizontal plane, help you (and the audience) feel centered and composed.

- Open arms signal inclusion.

- Hands touching the face, head, or hair make you look nervous or tentative—as does the "fig leaf" gesture in which hands are grasped together in front of the groin area.

- Hidden hands make you look less trustworthy.

- Gestures above your shoulders come across as erratic and overly emotional.

7. *Move*   Human beings (males, most especially) are drawn to movement. Movement keeps an audience from becoming bored. It can be very effective to move toward the audience before making an important point, and away when you want to signal a break or a change of subject. But don't move when you are making a key point. Instead, stop, widen your stance, and deliver the message.

8. *Monitor the Audience*   Keep reading the audience. Are they engaged or bored? If you see their interest flagging (increased texting, glancing at watches, and so on) do something unexpected: pause abruptly, change your voice level or tempo, ask a question, or involve the audience in an exercise.

One Small Nod

I've seen this with hundreds of audiences: when people connect with a message, they respond with a single nod. It's unconscious, and it's universal. See for yourself. When you are speaking, it's easy to tell if you've really connected. Watch for that one small nod.

Of course, the most important response to monitor is the audience's emotional reaction to your message. If you are announcing a large-scale organizational change, prepare to see a wide range of body language. And expect much of it, at least initially, to be negative.

Freeze, Flight, Fight

Change jerks us out of our comfort zones, activating the amygdala, which heightens the emotions of fear and anxiety and triggers the body's "freeze, flight, or fight" response. Signs of the amygdala's influence show up almost immediately after a major change is announced, and if you watch carefully, you will see people's body language reflect these responses.

Freezing is the body's first line of defense against threat or danger. And in organizational transformation there are obvious threats: people are afraid of the unknown, afraid of failure, afraid of appearing to be or actually being inadequate to face the new challenges. There is also the very real potential for loss—of current workplace relationships, the value of current competencies, the current rate of compensation, and (in some cases) even employment. No wonder so many people's first inclination is to freeze in place when hearing about the next restructuring.

The threat inherent in change also causes people to respond by becoming as inconspicuous as possible. They will breathe shallowly (or even hold their breath); withdraw their jaws by tucking their chins; raise their shoulders toward the ears, causing the neck to look shorter (the opposite of "sticking one's neck out"); avoid eye contact; draw their arms close to their bodies; and minimize hand gestures. I've even seen people literally sink lower in their chairs in order to avoid detection.

Preparing for flight is the body's second option for action. Here the urge is to get far away from the situation. This can be reflected in a variety of distancing and disengagement behaviors. People may turn away, lean away, use objects as barriers, cross their arms and legs, or point their feet toward the nearest exit. You will also notice an increase in eye blocks—people rubbing or closing their eyes. Eye-blocking behaviors are so hardwired that children who are born blind will cover their eyes when they hear things they don't like.

Except for those who choose to resign, actual flight is not a viable option (most people can't dash out of a meeting room), and to compensate, people will increase pacifying behaviors in order to sooth or calm themselves. Pacifiers are used on a daily basis, but with limbic system arousal, they greatly accelerate. Expect to see people exhibit more self-touching—hand wringing, hair twirling, leg rubbing, temple massaging, lip touching, and so on.

Neck touching is one pacifier that differs between men and women. Women will lightly touch the side of their neck, cover the notch at the base of the neck, or play with a necklace. Men will more robustly grasp the front of the throat near the Adam's apple.

Fight (or active resistance) is the body's final tactic. Teeth clench, jaws jut out, eyes narrow, faces turn red, and hands curl into fists. Displays of aggressive body language include puffing out the chest and violating another person's space. Anger about to turn into rage is indicated by nose wings that start to dilate as the person oxygenates before going into action.

And You Thought Board Meetings Were Dull

One CEO wrote in another executive's performance review that he didn't appreciate the man's "negative body language," and threatened to fire him if he didn't stop pretending to shoot himself in the mouth with his finger every time the CEO proposed an initiative.

WHAT DO PEOPLE WANT FROM YOU?

Let's play a game. Here are the rules: we'll be asked to split a sum of money. I get to make the split, and you get to choose whether to accept or reject the split. If you reject it, both of us will walk away empty-handed.

Rationally, I should realize my advantage and offer a lopsided split in my favor, and you should accept the uneven split—because any amount of money is better than nothing. Right?

Wrong. If we're like everyone else who plays the game, we'll end up with an even split. Although the fairness of the split shouldn't logically affect the second player's decision, it nearly always does. If offered a lopsided split, the second player will reject the deal, and neither player will get any money.

To find out why people react in this way, a team of Princeton researchers attached players to fMRI machines. They discovered that when people are offered an unfair split, a primal part of their brains known as the anterior insula sends out signals of disgust and anger.[11] It doesn't matter one little bit that rejecting the split—regardless of how unfair—is an irrational financial decision. It feels right.

A close look at the psychology of relationships reveals that most individuals automatically attempt to keep a mental balance between what they contribute to a relationship and what they get back from it. When employees believe that they are putting more into their company than they are getting back, or when they do not perceive the distribution of rewards to be equitable, engagement slips dramatically.

When employees look for balance through equitable treatment, it is their *perception* of the treatment, rather than the treatment itself, that defines reality. And this perception is often created by what I refer to as the "symbolic behaviors" of leaders. The CEO of a chemical manufacturing company put it this way: "As a leader you must make it a routine part of your decision-making process to ask the question: Will this action be perceived as equitable?"

Your every action counts—so if you typically eat lunch with other executives in a special dining area, park your car in a reserved space, and don't rein in your own spending when asking lower-level employees to make cost cuts, the inequity symbolized by your behavior can demotivate the workforce and derail a major change initiative.

THE POWER OF EMPATHY

A few years ago, I conducted a research project for a regional president who had recently taken on his new position. "I am replacing a man who had been with the company for twenty years," he said. "I'm new to the organization, and I'd like you to find out what employees need from me as their leader."

A week later, I gave him my report. "I think you're going to like what I found," I began, "because what employees need most won't cost you anything. People aren't asking for additional pay or more support from headquarters. What they are waiting for—and what they want from you more than anything else—is a validation of their emotions and your acknowledgment of their distress." The employees in his division were waiting for the new leader to say to them, "You've lost a leader who was your friend, mentor, and model. What a difficult time you must be having! I can only imagine how tough this is on you."

Empathy is a powerful tool during transitions. People are more likely to hang on to the fear, uncertainty, and other negative emotions that major change brings if it seems to them that management has no clue about what they are feeling. Your team members don't expect you to solve all their problems and address all their concerns. But when people react emotionally to change, they want your respect, empathy, and understanding—which is why it is imperative that you identify and respond to their nonverbal cues.

It's only after a person's negative emotional reaction has been validated and allowed expression that he or she can begin to focus on the potential benefits and opportunities that are also inherent in any change. It is only after being allowed to mourn and honor the past that people can release it and begin to look to the future. And at that point, people need leaders who model optimism and a positive attitude—and, by doing so, inspire others to take action and to believe that they can and will succeed.

4

COLLABORATION

Body Language Cues for Inclusion

Sharon entered the conference room, took her place at the head of the table, put down her coffee cup, opened her laptop, greeted her new management team with remarks about the importance of collaboration, and asked individuals to introduce themselves. She had worked previously with some of the managers there, and she nodded, smiled, and made eye contact with each before calling the meeting to order. But then, as other team members began to speak, she seemed to lose interest in what was going on; she frequently looked away to check her computer screen, walked over to the coffee table for a refill, and, when her cell phone buzzed, excused herself to answer—at length. Then she announced a break, during which she asked me, in all seriousness, for a critique of her leadership style.

I wish I'd had this chapter to give her instead!

Critical elements of a company's competitiveness are the potential of its people, the quality of the information those people possess, and their willingness to share knowledge with others in the organization. The leadership challenge is to link these components as tightly as possible to facilitate increased collaboration and knowledge sharing in teams, in departments, and right across the company.

This chapter will explain how we are hardwired to connect with colleagues, how mirroring creates empathy, what the body language of inclusion means, how damaging the exclusion of individuals can be, the importance of how you say what you say, the importance of space, a new definition of "dress for success," what your office says about you, and why familiarity breeds collaboration.

THE UNIVERSAL NEED FOR COLLABORATION

One of my most requested speaking topics is "Harnessing the Power of Collaboration." The topic's popularity stems from corporate clients around the world realizing that the "silo mentality" and knowledge-hoarding behaviors are wasting the kind of collective brainpower that could save their organizations billions. Or lead to the discovery of a revolutionary new process or product. Or, in the current economic climate, help keep the company afloat when others are sinking!

And it's not just corporate profits that suffer when collaboration is weak: the workforce loses something too.

Individuals lose the opportunity to work in the kind of inclusive environment that energizes teams, releases creativity, and makes working together both productive and joyful.

Ouch! You Excluded Me

Naomi Eisenberger, a social neuroscience researcher at the University of California, Los Angeles, designed an experiment to find out what goes on in the brain when people feel rejected by others.[1] She had volunteers play a computer game while their brains were scanned by fMRI machines. Subjects thought they were playing a ball-tossing game over the Internet with the two other people. There was an avatar (a computerized graphic that represents a person in a virtual environment) for the volunteer, and avatars for two other people.

About halfway through this game of catch, the subject stopped receiving the ball, and the two other players threw the ball only to each other. In reality, there were no other human players, only a computer program designed to exclude the test subject at some point. But even when they learned the truth, the players said they still felt angry, snubbed, or judged, as if they had been left out of the game for some personal reason.

Even more interesting to the neuroscientists was what was happening in the subjects' brains. When people felt excluded, there was corresponding activity in the dorsal portion of the anterior cingulate cortex—the neural region involved in the "suffering" component of pain. In other words, the feeling of being excluded provoked the same sort of reaction in the brain that physical pain might cause.

As the research highlights, it really doesn't take much to make people feel left out. The nonverbal signals that make someone feel unimportant are often slight: letting your gaze wander while he or she is talking, or angling your shoulders even a quarter-turn away. Trivial actions (like Sharon's behavior with her new team), if they happen only infrequently, are most likely not going to demoralize a team member. But if you are continually offhanded, neglectful, or unresponsive to certain individuals, your behavior will not go unnoticed, and it can be seriously destructive of the collaboration you are seeking to foster in the group. It can also be very hurtful. Team members who feel that they and their ideas are being ignored will simply withdraw and stop contributing, and the sense of unease created by that withdrawal will broadcast itself subliminally to the whole group. Leaders with inclusive body language create an emotional environment that supports collaboration and high performance. But when a leader appears to play favorites by using more positive nonverbal signals with some people than with others, when a leader's body language excludes an individual, and when those behaviors result in "hurt" feelings—the pain is very real.

A Hunger for Connection

"Loneliness and the feeling of being unwanted is the most terrible poverty."

—*Mother Teresa*[2]

WIRED TO CONNECT

The roots of cooperation go back to our prehistory as a matter of survival. Belonging is not only a motivating component of workplace collaboration but also the brain's key driver. Our brains have evolved to be social and collaborative—constantly assessing what others may think or feel, how they are responding to us, whether we feel safe with them, and whether they feel safe with us.

Social animals thrive together—not separately. We have a need for belonging that is powerful and primitive. We love contributing, and we love being thanked. When others show us respect and appreciation, it triggers the same centers in the brain that are activated when we eat chocolate or have sex. Understanding this dynamic gives you insight into the intrinsic rewards of collaboration—and why it is so important that your body language signals are open and positive.

Mirror Neurons

As noted in Chapter Three, empathy can be a powerful motivator in the workplace. The field of neuroscience that holds the most promise for understanding collaborative leadership is the study of mirror neurons and how empathy develops in the brain. In the late 1980s, researchers at the University of Parma in Italy found that the brain cells of macaque monkeys fired in the same way whether they were making a particular motion (such as reaching for a peanut) or watching another monkey or human make that movement. In terms of motor cell activity, the monkey's brain could not tell the difference between actually doing something and seeing it done. The scientists named those brain cells "mirror neurons."[3]

You can spot mirror neurons in action when a newborn baby looks up and the mother smiles at him or her. We now know that if you monitored the infant's brain, mirror neurons would have fired on seeing the mother's smile—and those cells would have created the same pattern as they would if the baby had actually smiled. And indeed, within the first hours of life, the infant will begin to mimic those maternal smiles.

In an organizational context, employees search for cues from leaders and mimic their behaviors, both consciously and unconsciously. A key insight from mirror neuron research is the reinforcement of an old management truism: modeling desirable behaviors will encourage employees to follow suit. If you want your team to collaborate, then first you need to become a positive example of collaboration. Or as Mahatma Gandhi said, you need to "be the change you want to see in the world."

Before the discovery of mirror neurons, it was generally believed that we used analytical thought processes to interpret and predict other people's motives and actions. Now, however, the prevailing theory is that we understand each other not by analysis but, as mentioned in previous chapters, through emotion. In human beings, mirror neurons not only simulate actions but also reflect intentions and feelings. They thus play a key role in our ability to socialize and empathize with others. By reading body language signals (especially facial expressions) and automatically interpreting the emotion behind them, we get an intuitive sense of the world around us—without having to think about it.

Here's how it works in a corporate setting. Mirror neurons fire when you see an emotion expressed on a team member's face—or read it in his or her gestures or posture. You then subconsciously place yourself in the other person's "mental shoes" and begin to recall and experience that same emotion. It's your mirror neurons that give you the capacity to experience the joys and sorrows of others and to connect with them on an emotional level. When as a leader you mirror team members' facial expressions and body positions, you instantly communicate empathy and signal that you understand the feelings of the people around you and will take those feelings into account as you decide how to respond. This also explains why mirroring and the resultant feeling of being "connected" are such powerful parts of building a collaborative team.

Since the discovery of mirror neurons, various studies have been conducted to validate their effect. In a recent experiment, volunteers were (ostensibly) asked for their opinions about a series of advertisements. A member of a research team mimicked half the participants, taking care not to be too obvious. A few minutes later, the researcher "accidentally" dropped six pens on the floor. Participants who had been mimicked were two to three times more likely to pick up the pens. The study concluded that mimicry had not only increased goodwill toward the researcher (in a matter of minutes) but also prompted an increased social orientation in general.[4]

Synchrony and Cooperation

At a leadership conference last year, the meeting was opened by a group of drummers who led the entire audience in synchronous drumming. It was a great choice for a meeting intended to enhance collaboration. If that seems odd to you, consider the following. . . .

Marching, singing, dancing (and drumming) are all examples of activities that lead group members to act in synchrony with each other. Stanford University conducted research that showed that synchronous activity motivates members of a group to contribute toward the collective good. Across three experiments, people acting in synchrony with others cooperated more in subsequent group economic exercises, even in situations requiring sacrifice on a personal level from the group. Their results suggest that synchrony can increase cooperation by strengthening social attachment among group members.[5]

How Do You Listen?

As part of a research project, a group of undergraduate students at VU University Amsterdam watched an eight-minute film, after which they were asked to describe it as fully as possible to other students. The listeners were actually research assistants, and for half the participants they assumed a positive listening style (smiling, nodding, maintaining an open bodily position); for the other participants they assumed a negative listening style (frowning and unsmiling). Participants describing the film to positive listeners used more abstractions, describing aspects of the film that couldn't be seen, such as a character's thoughts and emotions. They also included more of their own opinions about what the film was trying to say. In contrast, participants speaking to negative listeners focused solely on objective facts and concrete details.[6]

The theory is that the smiles and nods of a listener signal interest and agreement, which in turn encourage the speaker to share more personal insights and speculation. Negative body language triggers a threat response that causes the speaker to pull back into the relative "safety" of facts.

What this means in the context of collaboration and leadership is that by merely adjusting his or her body language, a leader can actually influence how team members process and report information.

SIX BODY LANGUAGE TIPS FOR INCLUSION

The body language of inclusion is pretty much what you'd expect: it includes eye contact, smiling, head nods, and body orientation. But don't get fooled. These seemingly inconsequential behaviors are so powerful that they may dictate your success or failure as a collaborative leader. Here are six ways to use body language to enhance collaboration.

First Tip: Check Your Expectations

Pygmalion in the Classroom, one of the most controversial publications in the history of educational research, shows how a teacher's expectations can motivate student achievement. In this classic study, prospective teachers were given a list of students who had been identified as "high achievers." The teachers were told to expect remarkable results from these students, and at the end of the year, the students did indeed show sharp increases in their IQ test scores.[7]

In reality, these children had been chosen at random, not as a result of any testing. It was the teachers' belief in their potential that was responsible for the extraordinary results. The children were never told they were high achievers, but this message was delivered subtly and nonverbally through such behaviors as facial expressions, gestures, touch, and spatial relationships (the distance between teacher and student).

This self-fulfilling prophecy isn't only operational in the classroom. Tel Aviv University professor Dov Eden has demonstrated the power of the Pygmalion effect in all sorts of work groups, across all sectors and industries. It almost sounds too simple to be true, but Eden found that if supervisors or managers hold positive expectations about the performance of the people they lead, that performance will improve.[8]

Collaboration is based on trust and empowerment, and your willingness to trust and empower team members depends on whether you believe they will be able to take on that responsibility and succeed. Your expectations (and the way those expectations are broadcast through your body language) are a key factor in how well people perform on your team.

Second Tip: Activate Your Smile Power

A genuine smile not only stimulates your own sense of well-being but also tells those around you that you are approachable, cooperative, and trustworthy. A genuine smile comes on slowly, crinkles the eyes, lights up the face, and fades away slowly. In contrast, a counterfeit or "polite" smile comes on quickly and never reaches the eyes.

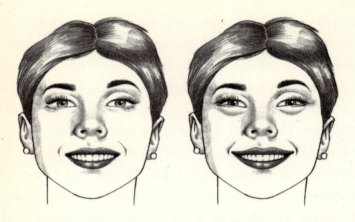

A polite smile   *A genuine smile*

Some nonverbal behaviors can bring out the best in people. Smiling is one of them. It makes you feel good and produces positive physiological changes in your body temperature and heart rate. But, most important for a collaborative leader, smiling directly influences how other people respond to you. When you smile at someone, he or she almost always smiles in return. And because facial expressions trigger corresponding feelings, the smile you get back actually changes that person's emotional state in a positive way.

Third Tip: Use Your Head

Collaboration depends on participants' willingness to speak up and share their ideas and insights. Your nonverbal signals can either increase participation or shut it off.

The next time you are in a meeting where you're trying to encourage a team member to continue speaking, nod your head using clusters of three nods at regular intervals. I've found that people will talk much more than usual when the listener nods in this manner.

Head tilting is another signal that you are interested, curious, and involved. The head tilt is a universal gesture of giving the other person an ear. As such, head tilts can be very positive cues when you want to encourage people to expand on their comments.

Fourth Tip: Look at People When They Speak

Eye contact is a powerful motivator to encourage speaking, because people feel that they have your attention and interest as long as you are looking at them. The power of eye contact to direct a conversation is evident even when the "listener" is a robot.

Scientists from Carnegie Mellon University, in collaboration with researchers from Japan's Osaka University and from ATR Intelligent Robotics and Communication Laboratory, found that a robot's eye movement is key to guiding the flow of a conversation with more than one person. The robot (called Robovie) used for the experiments was given the ability to combine gaze with speech.

Having been programmed to play the part of a travel agent, Robovie was able to control the flow of a booking negotiation quite effectively with strategic eye contact.

When it looked equally at two people, they took turns speaking. Those at whom Robovie only glanced spoke less, and those who were ignored completely spoke the least. This pattern was consistent about 97 percent of the time.[9]

As a leader, you set the tone for the meeting. Body language that signals boredom or disinterest will ensure that team members are disinclined to share their knowledge and viewpoints. If you want someone to speak up, avoid the temptation to check your text messages, your watch, or how the other participants are reacting. Instead, focus on whoever is speaking to make sure that he or she feels that you are listening.

Fifth Tip: Use the "Ultimate Connective Gesture"

When you make an uplifting statement (for example, "This is a wonderful opportunity"), gesture toward the listener with an upward open palm and then casually pull your hand back toward your body. In the example, you would start your gesture toward the other person as you say the word "wonderful" and bring the gesture toward you as you say the word "opportunity." When you do this, you are nonverbally connecting the two of you in the most positive and inclusive way.

Sixth Tip: Remove Barriers

Face people directly. Even a quarter-turn away creates a barrier (the "cold shoulder"), signaling a lack of interest and causing the speaker to shut down. Physical obstructions are especially detrimental to the effective exchange of ideas. Take away anything that blocks your view or forms a barrier between you and the rest of the team. Close your laptop, turn off your cell phone, put your purse or briefcase to the side.

And if you think it makes you look more efficient (or important) to be continually checking your laptop or cell phone for messages, think again. As one member of a management team recently told me, "There's this senior exec in our department who has a reputation of being totally addicted to his BlackBerry. He is constantly on the machine during internal meetings. When he finally focuses on others, peers make jokes about his 'coming back to earth.' We know he's not tracking the conversation because he keeps asking questions that have been already responded to. The result is that when he does contribute, he has no credibility."

Even at a coffee break, be aware that you may create a barrier by holding your cup and saucer in a way that seems deliberately to block your body or distance you from others. A very successful senior executive (who happened to be a body language aficionado) once told me he could evaluate his team's comfort by how high they held their coffee cups. It was his observation that the more insecure an individual felt, the higher she held her coffee. People with their hands held at waist level were more comfortable than those with hands chest high.

Most of all, remember that team members will be watching you all the time, and they will be waiting to see if your behavior is congruent in both formal and informal settings. When one CEO hosted a corporate function designed to gather ideas from participants, he listened attentively during the presentations, but spent the breaks sitting far away from the group, reading a newspaper. It was only natural shyness that caused him to withdraw, but by now I'm sure you can accurately guess how the other people in the group evaluated his behavior.

THE IMPORTANCE OF HOW YOU SAY WHAT YOU SAY

Joan got a call from her boss, Shelly. "I knew from the sound of her voice when she said hello and asked how I was that someone else got the promotion I was up for," Joan told me. "I also knew that Shelly was unsure about her decision."

How did Joan know those things from just the sound of a few neutral words?

Paralinguistic communication, also known as vocal body language, is the answer. Volume, pitch, inflection, pace, rhythm, rate, intensity, clarity, pauses—all of these play a role in how you say what you say—and that "how" can sometimes be more revealing of your true meaning than the "what" contained in the words.

Sued for the Sound of Your Voice?

In 2002, Nalini Ambady made audiotapes of physicians and their patients in session. Half of the doctors had been previously brought to court for malpractice. She played the tapes for her students, who were able to determine which physicians had been sued. But here's the catch: the recordings were "content-filtered." All that the students could hear was a low-frequency garble. But based on the intonation alone, they could distinguish one group from the other. The doctors who had been sued had a dominant, hostile, less empathic style, whereas the other group sounded warmer.[10]

Leaders must therefore keep in mind that when they speak, their listeners won't only be evaluating their words; they will also be automatically "reading" their voices for clues to possible hidden agendas, concealed meanings, disguised emotions, unexpected surprises—anything, in short, that will help them determine whether or not they can rely on what they're being told. Your voice is as distinctive as your fingerprint. It conveys subtle but powerful clues into feelings and meanings. Think, for example, about how tone of voice can indicate sarcasm, concern, or confidence. Or how an increase in volume and intensity grabs attention because of the heightened emotion (passion, anger, assertiveness, certainty) it signals.

The limbic brain, where emotions are processed, also plays the primary role in processing vocal cues. Researchers from the University of Geneva in Switzerland discovered that they could tell whether a subject had just heard words spoken in anger, joy, relief, or sadness by observing the pattern of activity in the listener's brain.[11]

The effect of paralinguistic communication is so potent that it can, for example, make bad news actually sound palatable or, conversely, take all the joy out of a positive message. I've seen managers give unflattering feedback while still exhibiting warm feelings through their tone of voice—and those who were being critiqued still felt positively about the overall interaction. I've also seen managers offer words of praise and appreciation in such a flat tone of voice that none of the recipients felt genuinely acknowledged or appreciated.

In collaborative assignments, you are asking people to put aside their personal agendas and egos in the service of collective solutions that benefit the entire organization. For there to be any chance of this happening, team members have to know that the leader is 100 percent committed to their success. So when you say that you trust, support, and believe in your team, you'd better sound as though you mean it.

Speech Convergence

One of the most intriguing aspects of vocal behavior is speech convergence—the way people adopt the speech patterns and voice qualities of those whom they admire and want to be like. In fact, influence in an organization can be predicted by analyzing speech patterns. Those individuals who have the greatest effect on the greatest number of people (in terms of changing their speaking style) will also have the most control of the flow of information within the organization. So when you find the people in your organization who cause the most speech convergence, you also find the informal leadership.

Speech convergence can also be used as a technique to help people understand your message. The more adept you are at altering your speed, volume, and tone to match that of the group you are addressing, the better they will hear and accept what you have to say.

USING SPACE

Proximity is the measurable distance between two people. We keep different distances depending on the types of relationships we have with others. In North America, the intimate zone (0–18 inches) is reserved for those with whom we have close personal relationships—family and loved ones. The close personal zone (18 inches–2 feet) is the space that friends and trusted business colleagues can occupy. The far personal zone (2–4 feet) is the distance at which we feel most comfortable dealing with team members and business colleagues. The social zone (4–12 feet) is where the majority of our professional dealings take place and where we interact with new business acquaintances. The public zone (over 12 feet) is used mostly for public speaking. We unconsciously monitor these spatial zones, and we automatically adjust as we interact with various people and as a relationship evolves.

Reserved for loved ones and very close friends

Friends welcome

Team members invited

Where business relationships begin

Used for formal presentations

Broadly speaking, we tend to stand closer to those we like (or expect to like), who interest us, whom we trust, or whom we want to get to know. When you form a new team, people will initially interact in the social zone. However, as the group begins to gel—as they get to know and trust one another—you can see them move physically closer.

I always notice the amount of space my clients use with me. As they shorten the distance between us, I know that I am moving from being treated as a vendor to being seen as a trusted adviser.

When people are not aware of these zones and the meanings attached to them, unintentional violations can occur. For example, highly confident and powerful people typically occupy greater personal space, which may result in their infringing on another person's territory.

Space invasions are better tolerated when the invader is attractive or of high status. But people's territorial responses are primitive and powerful. When someone uninvited comes too close, it automatically triggers an increase in the heart rate and galvanic skin response (sweat gland activity and changes in the sympathetic nervous system) of the invadee. You can tell if you have infringed on people's space by the way they react—stepping away, withdrawing their head or neck, or angling their shoulders away from you.

Managers who stand over an employee who remains seated during a conversation risk causing the employee to feel subjugated or overpowered, creating a vague discomfort—however positive the actual words being said.

There are other kinds of territorial invasion as well. These include leaning on, touching, or standing close to another person's possessions—desk, computer equipment, furniture, and so on. Even leaning against a wall in someone's office or blocking a doorway can come across as dominating or intimidating.

It isn't only professional relationships that can suffer from unwanted space invasion. One night not long ago, when I was traveling on business, I had dinner at an oceanside resort, and I noticed a man and a woman seated across the room. The couple sat framed by a large picture window, while the setting sun turned the sky shades of yellow, orange, magenta, and deep purple. It was a beautiful image. But then I began to observe the couple's body language.

During the course of the meal, I watched the man lean toward the woman—and saw her respond by pulling away from him. He leaned toward her again—and again she pulled away. The more the man leaned forward, the more his dinner companion tilted back. By dessert, he was almost sprawled across the table, and she was practically falling backwards off her chair. I couldn't hear a word they were saying, but it was perfectly obvious that whatever he was proposing, she wasn't signing on.

The funny part was, the man seemed totally oblivious to the nonverbal signals the woman was so clearly sending. He would have been much more successful if he had (literally) backed off.

Seating Arrangements

In most of the meetings you attend, the seating arrangement may not be an issue. But it can make a big difference in a collaborative session. I'm not suggesting that you use place cards for attendees, but you should be aware that strategic positioning is an effective way to obtain cooperation—and that neglecting this dynamic can inhibit your collaborative goals.

There are two power positions at any conference table—the dominant chair at the head of the table facing the door and the "visually central" seat in the middle of the row of chairs on the side of the table that faces the door. Choosing the dominant chair may be the most effective way for a leader to control the agenda or dominate the meeting, but it also stifles collaboration. When the leader takes this spot, ideas are then directed to him or her for validation (or rejection) rather than to the entire group. So take a moment before your next meeting and think about the relationship you want to establish with team members. Then choose your seat accordingly: sit at the head of the table or at the midpoint on the side if you want to exert control, and choose any other position around the table if you want to state symbolically that you are an equal member of a collaborative team.

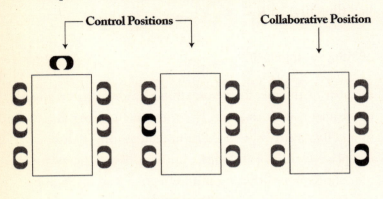

Where you sit sends a message.

Seating positions may even help create leaders. For example, it's been noticed that people who sit at either end of the table in a jury room are more likely to be elected foreman and that persons in visually central positions (that midpoint previously mentioned) are also more likely to be perceived as leaders. In the jury scenario, choice of foreman is mainly about the symbolism of the head-of-the-table position; with the central position, it is more about the power of eye contact: because the person seated in this central location is able to maintain eye contact with the most group members, he or she will be able to interact with more people and, as a result, will most likely emerge as the leader. (So if you wanted to enhance the leadership credibility of a junior team member, it would be wise to seat him or her in one of these two positions.)

Have you ever noticed that when two people sit at a table, they often choose chairs on opposite sides? This is automatically adversarial in terms of territory—the kind of seating arrangement that divorce attorneys and their clients typically adopt. Groups of people may also sit on opposite sides of a conference table and unwittingly divide into an "us and them" mentality. If you intentionally mix up the seating arrangements (or hold your meeting at a round table—or forego the table and simply place chairs in a circle), you can discourage the tendency to "take sides."

Sitting at right angles is the arrangement most conducive to informal conversation. Sitting side by side is the next best. This is important to remember if you want to foster personal ties between team members. The outcome of any collaborative effort is dependent on well-developed relationships among participants. People are naturally reluctant to share information with others when they don't know them well enough personally to evaluate their trustworthiness. So if you notice that the same people are taking the same seats at every meeting, rearrange the seating to stimulate conversation and encourage new relationships to develop.

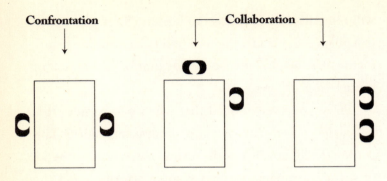

Seating invites confrontation or collaboration.

If you want to accelerate collaboration after a merger, you might try something like what Sujit Patil of Tata Chemicals Limited describes here: "We experimented with a unique process during the integration meeting after one of our early M&As, where seating arrangement during employee integration made a positive difference. We arranged chairs in concentric circles, rather than in a theatre style or around a conference table that might have made one group seem dominant. This very subtle nonverbal communication was very powerful and ensured a feeling of equality among the managers from both the organizations. The participation level was much higher."

Have a Seat—but Not There

"The Project Manager introduced a new consultant. The new guy smiled and shook hands with everybody, but it looked like an insincere, almost condescending smile and the handshake was soft and slippery. That was his first mistake. His next—and last—was sitting in the chair of a technical leader who was away on vacation. After that, the entire team boycotted the consultant, and his contract was quietly terminated after a couple of weeks. Nobody cared about his skills or contribution to the project."

—*E-mail from an engineer*

DRESS FOR SUCCESS

The senior executive came in wearing a designer suit, white shirt, and power tie. He checked the time on his Rolex wristwatch and placed his elegant briefcase on the table. He exuded authority, power, and status, and would have been perfectly dressed for a board of directors function. But that wasn't the kind of meeting he was chairing.

He had assembled a multilevel, multifunctional group—a diagonal slice of thirty people from across the organization—and had taken them off-site for two days to cocreate the necessary steps for achieving the company's new strategic plan. The hope was that collaboration and knowledge sharing would begin at this meeting and expand from here into every department.

It wouldn't be easy. The theme was "We're all in this together"—already a touchy subject, as the employees knew there would be cutbacks in spending and employee numbers. (And few expected that "together" meant that executives would also be asked to cut costs and reduce their ranks.)

But despite some initial reluctance on the part of the attendees, the first day had gotten off to a good start. Told to come dressed comfortably, most people were in jeans or slacks with polo or tee shirts. Consultants hired to facilitate the event had done a good job warming up the group and helping them begin to bond.

Then the senior exec came in to lead the meeting. From the moment he walked into the room, all hope for collaboration flew out the window. Not only was he making a late entrance (instead of arriving earlier that morning with the rest of the group), he didn't look like one of the team. He looked like a "suit," a hierarchical leader who would ask for input only as a rubber stamp for decisions he'd already made.

I'll never know why he chose to dress like that. Maybe he had a business appointment with an important client later that day, maybe he thought that this was the way a senior executive should always dress, or maybe he just didn't think it mattered. But as anyone who was there that day could tell you, it not only mattered but was pivotal.

If I could have caught him before he entered the room, I would have told him to take off his jacket, loosen his tie, and roll up his shirtsleeves. (I'd also have advised him to remove the Rolex and leave the Gucci briefcase on a chair in the corridor.) But, instead, all I could do was sit there and watch as resistance and skepticism built and rippled through the assembled group.

I think of this incident every time I hear the words "dress for success." As with every other piece of nonverbal communication, you need to first consider what "success" means in a particular context. Although there is absolutely nothing wrong with wearing an expensive suit and tie (in fact, it would be appropriate and advisable for almost any other executive function), you need to be aware of the message it sends. And if your goal is to support and model collaboration, then you need to realize that dressing like the other team members is the successful message in this situation.

WHAT YOUR OFFICE SAYS ABOUT YOU

Our brains are tuned to status. Michael Marmot, in his book *The Status Syndrome*, has shown that high status correlates with human longevity and health, even when income, education, and other environmental circumstances are factored in.[12] In short, we are biologically programmed to care about status because it favors our survival.

Which brings me to your office.

Because you are a leader, you already have acknowledged status in your organization, but there are many ways your office can reinforce that status. You can occupy the largest (or the corner) room, have a picture window with a great view, or sit behind a massive desk (obstructing a visitor's view of your lower body). You can choose a chair with armrests, a high back that tilts, a swivel seat, and rollers for feet. You can then put the visitor in a smaller, lower, and fixed chair on the opposite side of your desk. You can even seat visitors on a low sofa across the room and place a coffee table in front of them. Arranging your office in this manner allows you to control the space between you and others, keeping them at a distance and in essence saying that you won't come to them—they must come to you (and only if invited).

Projecting power, authority, and status may be a key part of your nonverbal strategy to impress potential clients, customers, and investors—and I often advise clients to think of their office space as a symbol of their (and their company's) prestige.

But when it comes to building collaboration within your organization, status cues like these send a conflicting, distinctly unwanted message. If creating a collaborative culture is essential to meeting your business objectives, then you might want to rearrange your office to reflect this. For example, seating people directly across from your desk places them in an adversarial position. Instead, place the visitor's chair at the side of your desk, or create a conversation area (chairs of equal size set around a small table—or at right angles to each other) and send signals of informality, equality, and partnership.

FAMILIARITY BREEDS COLLABORATION

In the 1960s, the University of Michigan psychologist Robert Zajonc demonstrated an important, subconscious relationship that exists between familiarity and "liking." Zajonc flashed up on a screen a sequence of irregularly shaped octagons, but ones too fleeting for the subjects watching to consciously register having seen them. He then showed those octagons again at a slower speed, together with a number of new ones, and asked his subjects to say which ones they "liked" best. Zajonc found that without exception they preferred the octagons they had been shown previously, even though they were unaware of having viewed them. He termed this phenomenon "the mere exposure effect."[13]

What has this to do with leadership and collaboration? Plenty.

There are two kinds of knowledge in your organization: explicit and tacit. Explicit knowledge is information that can be transferred in a document or entered in a database. Accessing tacit knowledge (insights, intuitions, things that "we don't know we know") requires a conversation and a relationship. The first building block of that relationship is "the mere exposure effect." Familiarity increases the likelihood that your team members will like one another and feel comfortable enough to share their thoughts and speculations.

So when you hold off-site retreats, organization-wide celebrations, or workplace events, make sure to provide plenty of opportunities for social activities and to schedule frequent and long breaks. The more your team members see each other and interact in informal ways, the more they will like each other and build the personal bonds that later translate into collaborative success.

■ ■

Today's corporation exists in an increasingly complex and ever-shifting ocean of change. Leaders therefore need to rely more than ever on the intelligence and resourcefulness of their staff. Collaboration is not a "nice to have" leadership philosophy. It is an essential ingredient for organizational survival and success based on the essential truth that none of us is smarter than all of us.

5

COMMUNICATING VIRTUALLY AND FACE-TO-FACE

Close Encounters of the Business Kind

Chip is the head of a privately owned, highly successful financial services firm whose associates and research fellows are spread out around the globe. The corporate headquarters are in upstate New York, but as Chip told me, "Sometimes I'm there alone, and sometimes it's just one other person and me. Oftentimes the offices are empty—as all of us may all be working from home or traveling to meet with clients."

His is a virtual organization, heavily dependent on technology for connection and collaboration. Of necessity, Chip utilizes an array of computer-mediated communication tools, including e-mail, wikis, blogs, and videoconferencing. And, of course, he is constantly using his BlackBerry for private conversations, teleconferences, and text messaging.

But even though his geographically dispersed organization is technologically equipped and connected, Chip also creates opportunities for face-to-face meetings. Once a week he hosts a dinner party with all local staff, and as often as possible he flies to international locations to do the same with staff there. Annually he gets his entire workforce together for a two-day strategic planning meeting, where he builds extra time for socializing into the agenda.

Why would a leader, whose company is so infused with technology, still invest the time, energy, and money to get employees together for all these face-to-face encounters?

This chapter will answer that question for leaders who head virtual enterprises or work mainly with virtual teams, and who are looking for means to balance technology-based and face-to-face interactions for maximum effectiveness. You will discover the specific advantages inherent in "lean" and "rich" communication media—and the nonverbal cues that are critical for success in each. You will learn which nonverbal signals in videoconferencing are interpreted differently from those encountered during "in person" meetings, how body language is becoming part of virtual reality, and how technology has produced a new generation of communication platforms that make body language savvy an increasingly important business skill. You will also discover the nonverbal cues that are exclusive to face-to-face communication—and why these cues are vital to creating personal relationships and building trust in a team, a department, or an organization.

TECHNOLOGY, THE GREAT ENABLER

Communication technology has completely changed the way we connect with people to conduct business. It has opened global markets and fostered the use of geographically dispersed teams—including multisite organizations and remote or home working. And the ability to connect virtually will become even more crucial as more employees work remotely and as complex tasks are broken down into smaller and smaller units to be managed and delivered by specialists (on teams or alone) who are linked by technology.

Communication options have never been greater—from instant messages to in-person meetings—and the question isn't "Which is best?" but "Which option works best for a particular purpose at a particular time?" The answer to that question, in large part at least, depends on whether the task at hand calls for a lean or a rich medium of communication.

Lean Communication

There are several categories into which communication technology can be divided. For example, communication modes are either synchronous (real-time interaction—like a phone call) or asynchronous (sent and stored information that people can access and post at different times—like a YouTube video). But from a body language perspective, the most important division is between lean and rich communication modes.

The following are examples of lean communication:

E-mail: asynchronous exchange of text with possible file attachments

Blog: frequent publishing of stream-of-consciousness writing with links to related material

Instant messaging (IM): exchange of text that appears almost immediately on the screens of users

Whiteboard: live, interactive sharing of digital writing and drawing tools

Wiki: server program that allows multiple users to develop the content of a Web site

There are obvious advantages to text-based communication tools. They are fast and inexpensive, and most employees have access to them and are comfortable using them. These tools can reach large audiences quickly, and they also create a written record of events, which can be valuable for tracking progress and for keeping everyone up-to-date. And there is a strong psychological advantage inherent in text-based communication as well—a kind of democratic leveling process. For example, in a document conference or Wiki, it will not be your age, gender, race, voice, or appearance that is under scrutiny; it will be your ideas, content, data, and presentation alone.

But, as you know, nonverbal cues are not simply vehicles for prejudice; they play an essential role in our understanding of interpersonal communication. This "behavioral invisibility" is in fact one reason why e-mail messages are so often misinterpreted. People too often misjudge the writer's emotional intent, especially if the message is poorly written (as they so often are!). As one executive put it: "If Mark Twain were sending an e-mail, you can be certain that the message, with all its nuances, would get through."

I've seen an overreliance on e-mail, the inappropriate use of "reply to all," and a failure to respond to messages, all leading to conflicts, misunderstandings, and the breakdown of trust. Because they lack the social signals that are so important for interpersonal bonding, lean communication tools are most effective when communication is more task related, such as when sharing guidelines and documents, rather than in the initial stages of the project when relationship building is key.

Then there is the isolation factor that can come as a result of a group's dependence on technology. Your team doesn't even have to be geographically separated to feel disconnected. According to Karen Sobel Lojeski, CEO of Virtual Distance International, geography can be a factor, but groups risk suffering the negative effects of "virtual distance" any time electronic communication becomes a substantial substitute for talking on the phone or meeting in person.[1] So if a team leader is located in the next cubicle but prefers to instant message rather than talk, that's virtual distance at work.

Richer Communication

Communication gets richer when you add voice, image, or both. One study published in the *Journal of Personality and Social Psychology* found that speakers, as compared to e-mail senders, were almost 40 percent better at communicating enthusiasm, skepticism, empathy, sympathy, irony, doubt, belief, encouragement, caution, and humor.[2] The following are a few examples of richer technology:

Telephone call: a one-on-one conversation

Teleconference: multiple participants on an audio connection using a phone, computer, or other device

Web presentation: audio plus screen sharing in which the presenter shares his or her computer screen with remote users

Podcast: a feed of new or updated multimedia content to which users subscribe

Videoconferencing: live, interactive audio and video connections between people at two or more sites

Virtual hallway or media space: always-on video and audio link between two or more sites

Richer media have an advantage in transmitting attitudes and emotions through vocal prosody (variations in stress, tone, timing, and pitch), facial expressions, body posture, and physical gestures. A Cisco Systems study, conducted by business psychologists at Pearn Kandola, evaluated the impact of lean and rich media on group effectiveness. Among their findings:[3]

- It takes a minimum of two weeks before relationships established through computer-mediated communication are as socially grounded as face-to-face relationships.

- The use of richer media (voice and video communications in particular) helps establish and build relationships.

- Trust, a critical factor in influencing group effectiveness, is more readily generated through high-quality, media-rich forms of communication.

- "Silence," or nonresponse to communication (e-mail, voice mail, and so on) leads people to misattribute explanations for this silence.

Videoconferencing

Videoconferencing is one of the richest communication technologies. But unless you are equipped with the very latest technology, such as Cisco's TelePresence (which I'll discuss later in this chapter), you may find that videoconferencing presents its own set of sometimes tricky challenges. For example, corporate networks that have not been upgraded will probably lack the bandwidth to make audio and video components work smoothly together. A speaker's lips and words will often be out of sync. Unexpected freeze-frames and annoying broken connections can play hell with participants' grasp of continuity and sense. IT technician burnout is an ever-present threat. And from the nonverbal perspective, there is the bothersome problem of what might be called "dysfunctional eye contact": because the camera and display screen are separate components, each time you look at the screen, you shift your eye from the camera. Someone watching you in a videoconference notices that you constantly look away. If the camera is above the screen, you always appear to be looking down. And, as you know, a lack of eye contact reduces trust, collaboration effectiveness, and satisfaction with the interaction.

The Myth of Multitasking

Technology has many advantages, but some devices that were designed to make us more productive are now creating a new set of productivity problems. When laptops, personal digital assistants, and cell phones are close by, attendees at workplace meetings struggle to keep their focus on the speaker. It's just too compelling and easy to check e-mail and text messages and to surf the Web instead. Of course these workers think that they are multitasking. But when it comes to its ability to pay attention, the brain focuses on concepts sequentially and not on two things at once. In fact, the brain must disengage from one activity in order to engage in another. And it takes several tenths of a second for the brain to make this switch. As John Medina, author of *Brain Rules*, says, "To put it bluntly, research shows that we can't multitask. We are biologically incapable of processing attention-rich inputs simultaneously."[4]

In addition, what seems like a harmless activity to the attendee sends a nonverbal message of disinterest and dismissal to the speaker. That's why some companies I've worked with have installed the "topless" meeting— banning all laptops, iPhones, BlackBerrys, and so on.

SIX TIPS FOR A CONFERENCE CALL

Teleconferencing adds the element of voice with all its nuances of pace, tone, volume, pauses, and inflection that give meaning to a spoken message. Because others can't see you, voice plays an even more important part in conference calls than in face-to-face conversations, and a manager's body language when speaking on the phone can affect the strength and intonation of his or her voice. Here are a few tips to keep in mind.

First Tip: Modulate Your Voice

Breathe from your diaphragm, and vary your vocal range and tone, avoiding a monotone delivery that sounds as if you are bored with the topic. Because of the many people who may be participating in the teleconference, it is also important to enunciate and speak clearly.

Second Tip: Stay Focused

Focus your eyes and attention on one place. If you shuffle papers, check e-mail, or let your gaze wander around the room, it detracts from your communication, even electronically.

Third Tip: Stand

Stand up, if possible, especially when you want to convey greater confidence. It will give your voice more energy and conviction.

Fourth Tip: Smile

Smile while you are talking—doing so will transmit energy and enthusiasm in your voice. If your voice sounds inviting, it will draw people out. And, as my husband (who was an actor and voiceover professional) reminds me, a key voiceover technique is "delivery with a smile."

Fifth Tip: Keep It Short

Because there is no visual feedback with which to check reactions, if people don't speak up, you can't be sure that they understand, agree, or have a problem with what was just proposed. So keep statements short and ask for frequent feedback.

Sixth Tip: Follow an Agenda

Send out an agenda ahead of time and stick to it. Make sure everyone knows the purpose of the call, how long it will last, and what they need to do to prepare for the call. Given that a conference call lacks the clarity of visual cues, it will go smoother with the added clarity of an agenda.

IMPORTANT TIPS FOR VIDEOCONFERENCING

Research has discovered that people process information differently if they receive it via videoconference rather than face-to-face. Participants in videoconferences tend to be influenced more by heuristic cues—such as how likeable they perceive the speaker to be—than by the quality of the arguments presented by the speaker.[5] This is due to the higher cognitive demands that videoconferencing places on participants. So if you are the presenter at a videoconference, you will want to emphasize nonverbal signals of likeability and warmth—leaning forward slightly, smiling, showing palms, and so on.

There are a few other tips to keep in mind. Because the sound system on a videoconference is sometimes less than ideal, you'll need to speak slowly and enunciate clearly. Remember that distracting mannerisms and facial expressions can all be picked up and exaggerated on camera. Maintain a "less is more" attitude: don't move around (stay seated or stand in one place), look at the camera to directly address the audience, and keep your hand gestures close to your body.

If you make your face clearly visible when you speak (on a monitor or in person), your audience will understand you faster, according to a recent study coauthored by Virginie van Wassenhove at the University of Maryland. Her research found that when your audience sees your face (and most especially your lips) clearly, they may actually be able to anticipate what you're going to say before you say it, speeding up communication.[6]

TECHNOLOGY BRINGS A NEW RANGE OF COMMUNICATION OPTIONS

The possibilities are endless: holographic technology that "transports" a person around the world, robots that read body language, cell phones that give you clues to a speaker's emotional state. Who knows which of today's experiments will become tomorrow's preferred communication channel? It's difficult to predict the future, but as promised at the chapter's beginning, here are two of today's technologies that all leaders should know about: Cisco's TelePresence and Linden Lab's Second Life.

TelePresence

Cisco Systems' TelePresence is one of a growing number of cutting-edge videoconference systems designed to replicate the feeling of an in-person meeting through state-of-the-art cameras, screens, lighting, and audio. TelePresence uses "life-size" high-definition video that displays the full upper body; it also employs directional sound technology, so you hear voices coming from the direction of individual participants.

Cisco's TelePresence

By creating a more natural, productive, and realistic experience, this new generation of videoconferencing makes participants feel as though they are actually sitting in the same room with people who are on the other side of the world. In reality, attendees might be located in several different countries, but the image projected of everyone sitting at the same conference table is so realistic that the impression of actually being in the same room is uncanny. Best of all, from a body language perspective, participants in a TelePresence conference are able to see how a negotiator responds to a demand, watch a leader lean forward to emphasize an important point, and observe fleeting glances of concern or head nods of agreement.

And if price has been an obstacle for your organization, now you don't even have to purchase the technology for in-house use. You can "reserve" it. Last year, two major hotel groups, Starwood Hotels and Resorts and Marriott International, announced the addition of public TelePresence suites in key cities worldwide.

Second Life

Second Life (launched in 2003) is one of a number of simulated 3-D Internet imitations that make up a virtual world in cyberspace in which humans interact (as avatars) with one another for social and economic transactions.

Businesswoman and her Second Life avatar

Although it may look like an online game, Second Life is a virtual world where "residents" can travel, socialize, create things, and even do business. College professors teach classes there, librarians set up "islands" to help people find resources, and well-known companies (Sears, Coca-Cola, Mazda, and Starwood Hotels among them) create their own islands where employees attend global meetings, collaborate on projects, and meet with clients. Both IBM and Intel have developed private collaboration spaces in Second Life. IBM has even gone so far as to establish a "virtual worlds conduct policy" for its employees.[7]

Leaders using Second Life should be aware that real-life body language "norms" still hold true (for example, female avatars will stand closer together than male avatars when conversing in virtual environments—just as humans do in real-life conversations). But the most intriguing nonverbal aspect of any of the cutting-edge virtual reality packages is that they allow participants to alter their digital self-representations dramatically and easily. And, as Stanford University researchers found out, when people change their self-representations, their behaviors also change (a reaction the researchers call "the Proteus Effect").[8]

In two studies, subjects were given avatars that were more attractive or taller than other avatars in the experiment. After less than one minute of exposure to their attractive avatars, subjects exhibited increased self-disclosure and were more willing to approach strangers of the opposite gender. In other words, the attractiveness of their "better-looking" avatars actually influenced their willingness to become more intimate with strangers. In the second study, participants who had taller avatars were more willing to make unfair splits in negotiation tasks than those who had shorter avatars, whereas participants with shorter avatars were more willing to accept unfair offers than those who had taller avatars. Almost instantly, the height of their avatars impacted how confident participants became.

Depending on how your team is using this technology—for collaboration, to build relationships in a dispersed team, to negotiate with clients—the way participants choose to represent themselves can have a dramatic impact on their interactions.

WHAT'S SO GREAT ABOUT FACE-TO-FACE?

Technology is pervasive, and travel is time consuming, expensive, and becoming more of a hassle every day. In addition, the planning needed to bring a group of people together (especially if your team or organization is globally dispersed) can be cumbersome. But, despite these drawbacks, many leaders (like Chip, the CEO you met at the beginning of this chapter) believe their businesses couldn't survive without face-to-face contact among the people of the organization.

A recent study by the *Harvard Business Review* confirms that most leaders put great importance on doing business in person—and link it directly to the bottom line. The study shows that 87 percent of professionals think that face-to-face meetings are essential for sealing the deal; 95 percent said it's the key to successful, long-lasting business relationships.[9]

Chip finds the time, energy, and expense he invests in personal contact worthwhile in terms of ROI. And he can't imagine his organization operating without these frequent, informal dinner parties. "You can get a lot from a phone call, an e-mail, or a videoconference, but there is nothing like actually getting together—especially for a meal and a drink—to really connect and get to know one another. It's fun and it recharges us. In fact, I view our deep personal relationships as a differentiating factor in the marketplace. It may well be the cornerstone of our success."

Any communication strategy takes skill. A well-crafted e-mail can be more effective than a poorly handled face-to-face meeting. But for the highest level of group engagement or to communicate any message that has an emotional component, you need to make a human-to-human connection. So if a leader is going to talk about new initiatives, major change, or strategic opportunities, or if he or she has to deliver bad news—my advice is always to do so in person.

As for building relationships, face-to-face is undeniably the most effective (and richest) communication medium and remains the most powerful human interaction. Technology may be bringing us closer to replicating the experience, but there is nothing yet that can fully replace the intimacy and immediacy of getting people together, face-to-face.

First Meetings—Personal and in Person

"Leadership communication is more about who you are than what you do or say. That's why I advise leaders to have that first meeting face-to-face, and to make it as personal as possible. Once someone has a sense of who you

> are, you can have productive conversations by
> phone or use effective email."[10]
> —*Terry Pearce, consultant and author of*
> Leading Out Loud

We were born with the innate capability to communicate through our postures, gestures, facial expressions, and vocal prosody. We may have spent years learning to read and write, but no one had to teach us to send and respond to nonverbal signals. In fact, our brains search for and expect these most primitive and significant channels of information. According to Dr. Thomas Lewis (an expert on the psychobiology of emotions and assistant clinical professor of psychiatry at the University of California, San Francisco), when we are denied these interpersonal cues, the brain struggles and real communication suffers.[11]

As advanced as the new wave of connective technologies is, there are (at least) two areas in which face-to-face remains superior: (1) informal encounters and (2) the most primitive and powerful nonverbal cue—touch.

Informal Encounters

Management by wandering around (MBWA) is familiar shorthand for a manager's physical presence and accessibility, a potent form of nonverbal communication.

This goes beyond an "open door" policy and takes managers out of their offices and into the workplace for those spur-of-the moment observations and interactions. The point of MBWA is to build the kind of relationships that can only happen when leaders really know the people who work for them. Here's an example from my book *This Isn't the Company I Joined.*[12]

At a claim office of about 125 employees, the head of human resources spent the day observing the local manager. Not only had the office ranked high on productivity, but this particular manager had received fantastic feedback on her company's Leadership Measurement survey. So the HR executive was curious to watch her interact with employees to figure out what generated this great response.

As they walked through the office, conversing about the normal work conditions, the manager would often stop and refer to specific individuals: "Steve over there has been in our area for fifteen years. Steve also coaches Little League. They won their game last Thursday."

Then they'd move on to someone else, and as they left that person's area, quietly the manager would say, "Sally had some problems with her daughter this year. You know how difficult teenagers can be. We've had many sessions behind closed doors where Sally's trying to sort through these problems."

Months later, when I interviewed the HR executive, that day at the claim office was still etched in her mind. "It became apparent to me," she explained, "that this manager knew all of her people. And I don't mean just knew their jobs. She knew each individual—their backgrounds and hobbies, what their concerns were, what got them excited. She knew when they were upbeat because things were going well, and she knew when they were struggling and needed her time and attention. I asked her how on earth she could do this for 125 people. Her response: 'That's my job.'"

It's not just managers who benefit from informal interactions. Employees congregating at the coffee station (or bumping into one another in the hallway) share information about "how things really get done around here." And when it comes to fostering collaboration and innovation, nothing can beat the spontaneous exchanges that occur when two people happen to encounter one another and strike up a conversation. As one very savvy CEO told me, "All the important talk at this conference takes place around the wine and cheese table."

High Touch

Several decades ago, John Naisbitt wrote a best seller (*Megatrends: Ten New Directions Transforming Our Lives*) in which he brought a new concept to the forefront. Called "high tech, high touch," the basic idea was that as humans became more capable of anonymous electronic communication, they would concurrently need more personal interaction.

Seems to me that Naisbitt was right on target—perhaps more literally than he knew.

Scientists have long studied nonverbal communication. But in recent years some researchers have begun to focus on a previously neglected and often more subtle kind of wordless communication: touch. Through this new focus, psychologists are coming to realize that even momentary touches can communicate an even wider range of emotion than hand gestures or facial expressions—and sometimes do so more quickly and accurately than words.

Physical contact is the most primitive and essential form of nonverbal communication we know. Touch, in fact, is so potent a force in early life that studies by the Touch Research Institute at the University of Miami consistently show that preterm babies who are touched or massaged grow faster and gain more weight than those who receive less touching.[13]

And the emotional power of a warm, friendly, or encouraging touch appears to retain its potency right into adulthood—a phenomenon explained chemically by the release of a hormone called oxytocin, which helps create a sensation of trust by reducing levels of the stress hormone cortisol. Or to put it more simply, touch makes you feel better.

The expression "That person is an easy touch" refers to the persuasive power of touch. In what has been labeled the "compliance effect," research has found that touch increases the likelihood that people will do what you request. Students who received a supportive touch on the back or arm from a teacher were nearly twice as likely to volunteer in class as those who did not.[14] And wait staff found that their tips increased (from an average of 11.5 to 14.9 percent) by adding a light touch on the shoulder when presenting patrons with the bill.[15]

The Emotional Touch

Some of the most intriguing experiments with touch, conducted by psychologists at DePauw University and the University of California, Berkeley, asked volunteers to communicate a list of emotions by touching a blindfolded stranger. The participants were able to communicate eight distinct emotions (from gratitude to anger to disgust to love), some with about 70 percent accuracy.[16]

In the United States, physical contact in the workplace is a hotly contested issue, and one that can bring charges of improper conduct—or worse. When allowed, touching in the context of business relationships tends to occur on the hands, arms, and back. But even though you need to use caution and good sense when using touch, I advise you not to avoid it.

Whether it is a handshake, a congratulatory high-five, or a supportive pat on the back, touch can become an essential part of business communication. We are programmed to feel closer to someone who's touched us. The person who touches also feels more connected. It's a compelling force, and even momentary touching can create a human bond. A touch on the forearm that lasts a mere fortieth of a second can make the receiver not only feel better but also see the giver as being kinder and warmer.

Try getting that response from a computer!

6

HE LEADS, SHE LEADS

Gender and the Body Language of Leaders

Let's say you divide a large work group into two teams. In the first group you assign a female leader, and in the second, a male. The two teams employ very different problem-solving strategies. In one, there is consensus and collaboration; in the other, clear direction and a hierarchical approach to decision making. If you didn't know which was which but had to guess, you'd probably say that the first team was led by the woman and the second by the man. And, most often (but not always), you'd be right.

When generalizing about any population segment—especially such large and diverse segments as "male" and "female"—there is bound to be a degree of inaccuracy and stereotyping. As you read this chapter, you will think of many individuals to whom the generalizations don't apply. Yet science has discovered some major gender differences in brain function, evolutionary predisposition, and communication style that can have a profound effect on the way men and women behave and are perceived in leadership roles.

This chapter explains the ways that gender can influence the body language of leaders. You will learn how the brains of men and women react differently to emotion and stress, how unconscious and unspoken reactions can undermine an emergent female leader, how followers evaluate the communication strengths and weaknesses of male and female leaders, and how to alter, accommodate, or modify your body language to be more effective.

THE NEUROSCIENCE OF GENDER

When it comes to brain research and gender, it's not a question of better or smarter—but it is a matter of difference. For example, men have approximately six-and-a-half times more grey matter related to cognitive functioning in the brain, and women have nearly ten times more white matter related to cognition than men have.[1] White matter connects brain centers in the neural network, whereas grey matter tends to localize brain activity into a single active brain center. Because of this difference, men tend to compartmentalize more brain activity and prefer to focus intently on one task at a time, whereas women's ability to integrate and assimilate information (aided by the fact that the female brain also has a larger corpus callosum—a thick band of fibers that connects the two brain hemispheres and facilitates their communication) gives them the edge in making crucial connections between seemingly disparate elements.

Until recently, differences in how men and women feel and express emotions were thought to be due to upbringing alone. But, according to Louann Brizendine, professor of clinical psychiatry at the University of California, San Francisco, emotional processing in the male and female brains is quite different.[2] In both genders, another person's emotional pain activates mirror neurons, but in the male brain, a second system (the temporal-parietal junction) quickly takes over, which in turn activates his "analyze-and-fix-it" circuits. So while the female brain is locked in emotional empathy, the male brain (having quickly identified the emotion) is busy searching for solutions.

Evolution programmed the male brain for hunting—which accounts for a man's narrower range of physical vision when compared with women, his ability to focus on a single source, and his better sense of direction (along with his reluctance to ask for directions when lost). Women have developed better peripheral vision, helping them take in multiple signals. Both genders stay alert for signs of danger—but, again, do so in their own unique ways: when entering a room, men automatically look for exits to estimate a possible escape, whereas women pay attention to people's faces to sort out who they are, how they feel, and whether it is safe to remain in their company.

Even women's propensity for crying has a partially neurological and physiological basis: the chromosomal development of prolactin in the female body and brain results in larger tear glands. So even in cultures where male tears are acceptable, women will produce more tears and cry more often.[3]

For decades, psychological research maintained that both men and women reacted to stress in the same physiological ways, meaning that when confronted with stress, individuals would either respond with aggressive behavior or withdraw from the stressful situation. Recently, however, neuroscientists have exposed a flaw in that assumption. Using fMRI, studies from University of Pennsylvania have discovered that men and women react to stress in very different ways.[4] In male brains, increased blood flow to the left prefrontal cortex did indeed suggest the activation of the "fight or flight" response. In women, however, stress activated the limbic part of the brain, which is associated with emotional responses. Women, they found, were more likely to manage their stress with what scientists have termed a "tend-and-befriend" response. When threatened, fearful, or stressed, women are more likely to protect and nurture others and to turn to family and friends for solace. This difference in giving and seeking social support during stressful periods seems to be the principal way men and women differ in their coping methods. But it is not the only difference.

Researchers at the University of Southern California, also looking at the divergent ways men and women's brains respond to stressful conditions, found a striking gender difference in brain function and how people evaluate emotions when under stress. The gender difference appeared in the brain regions that enable people to simulate and understand the emotions of others. According to the research, stress seemed to increase the capacity for empathy in women, whereas in males, stress reduced it.[5]

So what does all this science mean in the business arena? It means, for example, that in stressful and potentially threatening organizational challenges (a massive layoff, say, or a major departmental restructuring), it shouldn't surprise you if men on the leadership team tend to isolate and withdraw (working on "the numbers" to make it equitable for each department) while female leaders focus on addressing employees' concerns and distress. And although neither response is necessarily "better" in a given situation, these findings do suggest that a male-female balance on a leadership team would probably prove to be optimal in most situations.

WHY JANE DOESN'T LEAD

Before we look at the body language of male and female leaders, I want to tell you about some interesting research that offers an insight into why corporations have relatively few females in senior leadership positions. It has everything to do with body language—but not in the way you might anticipate.

Women have now crossed the 50 percent threshold and become the majority of the American workforce. They make up the majority of university graduates in the Organization for Economic Co-operation and Development (OECD) countries as well as the majority of professional workers in several rich countries, including the United States. And women already run many of the world's great companies, from PepsiCo in America to Areva in France.

There is also a genuine commitment in many organizations to develop the leadership abilities of female employees and to create workplace environments with family-friendly policies and flexible working arrangements—all in hopes of attracting, retaining, and grooming women for top management roles.

But despite the female majority in the workforce, women's strides in educational attainment, and an ongoing organizational effort in leadership development, relatively few females have made the journey all the way to the highest rungs of the corporate ladder. In fact, women number only 2 percent of the CEOs of the nation's Fortune 500 companies.

There is much speculation as to why this is so. For example, most research shows that people believe successful leaders need to have the characteristics typically

associated with men—although the actual qualities of
effective leadership are a combination of masculine
traits (forcefulness, self-confidence, task orientation)
and feminine traits (concern for people, feelings, and
relationships). An obvious consequence of this mistaken belief is that a man is more likely to be selected
for a leadership position than is an equally qualified
woman.

But there is another reason for the striking dearth
of female leadership at the corporate level: the difficulty
women find being subconsciously recognized by their
peers as acceptable leadership material.

Researchers at the University of Delaware compared
the nonverbal responses to male and female leaders
and found that intellectual assertiveness by women
in mixed-sex discussions elicits visible nonverbal cues
of negative affect. Females speaking up and taking a
leadership role receive fewer pleased responses and more
displeased responses from fellow group members than
male leaders offering the same input.

Here, with minor variations, is what the researchers
observed in team meetings: a woman states her opinion;
in response, negative nonverbal affect cues—frowns,
head shakes, eye contact avoidance, and so on—are
displayed, processed, and often mimicked by the entire
group to produce a less-than-positive consensus about the
value of the woman's contribution. And all of this occurs

without individuals on the team being aware of what's happening.[6]

At a time when conscious responses (for example, direct answers on questionnaires) are becoming less biased against women generally, unconscious responses to women asserting leadership behaviors continue to reflect discrimination from men and women alike. Because a person's hiring, salary, and promotion (especially to top leadership positions) often depend on her being recognized by all colleagues as an emergent leader, this reflexive, unconsidered response goes some way to explain why Jane doesn't lead even when she may be the best qualified to do so.

Keep these three key points in mind:

1. This was a study of leadership behaviors in peer groups. There is no evidence to suggest that women in formal leadership roles generate any greater negative (or less positive) emotional cues than do their male counterparts.

2. This was not about men discounting the contribution of women. The groups in the study had an equal mix of male and female members.

3. The power of nonverbal communication lies in its unconscious nature, so simply discussing this issue and bringing it to awareness will decrease its frequency and help nullify its effect.

THIRTEEN GENDER-BASED DIFFERENCES IN NONVERBAL COMMUNICATION

Colleagues Kate and Grant are part of a team sent to negotiate with a potential client. Grant thought the initial meeting went well, but Kate felt otherwise. While Grant was focused on the details of the business opportunity, Kate was picking up on the silent signals—the eye contact, the subtle emotional expressions, and shifts in body posture—that were being displayed by the members of the client team. These signals were telling her that the clients had some issues with their proposal.

Robert Rosenthal at Harvard University developed a test called the Profile of Nonverbal Sensitivity to analyze gender differences in decoding body language signals. The results showed that the ability to pick up and read body language is greater in females. With the exception of men who held jobs involving "nurturing, artistic, or expressive" work, females (from fifth grade to adulthood) had superior scores in accurately judging messages communicated by facial expressions, body movements, and voice quality.[7]

Women are not only more adept at identifying nonverbal cues but also better at expressing them—employing more animation, gesture, and vocal variety in their communication behavior. Women as a group react physically when something surprises or frightens them. (Men tend to be more controlled, more stoic.) But gender-influenced body language differences don't stop there. Here are a baker's dozen more:

1. Women are more comfortable when being approached from the front. Men prefer approaches from the side. Likewise, two men speaking will angle their bodies slightly, whereas two women will stand in a more "squared up" position—a stance that most men perceive as confrontational.

2. When a man nods, it means he agrees. When a woman nods, it means she agrees—or is listening to or empathizing with the speaker or encouraging the speaker to continue.

3. To a woman, good listening skills include making eye contact and reacting visually to the speaker. To a man, listening can take place with a minimum of eye contact and almost no nonverbal feedback.

4. Men who don't know each other well tend to keep a greater distance between them than women who have just met. As you saw in the previous chapter, this difference in interpersonal distance as determined by gender is present even in online communities (like Second Life).

5. In corporate settings, women and men use touch differently. Women use touch to signal agreement, sympathy, compassion, connection, and celebration. Touch among men is almost exclusively motivated by power—directed from the top down as a status marker.

(A manager can pat an employee on the back and say, "Good job," but the employee would hesitate to return the favor.)

6. Men expand into available space. They sprawl, sit with their legs spread or widely crossed, spread out their materials on a conference table, and stretch out their arms on the back of a chair. Women condense by keeping their elbows to their sides; tightly crossing their legs; stacking their materials in small, neat piles; and contracting their bodies to take up as little space as possible.

7. Women sound more emotional than men because they use approximately five tones when speaking—and their voices rise under stress. Men not only have a deeper vocal range but also use only approximately three tones. A man's deeper, louder voice is viewed as commanding and confident.

8. Men's propensity to minimize facial expressions causes uneasiness in women, who often perceive a lack of facial response as negative feedback. When a woman can't read the person she's talking to, she feels anxious.

9. Both sexes smile when genuinely happy or amused or when it is socially expected to do so, but women smile more often than men—to cover up uneasiness or nervousness or to take the sting out of a negative comment.

10. Men tend to express their anger nonverbally more than women do, and more quickly expel the anger through physical bursts of energy, such as by hitting a table.

11. Women stand with their legs close together, sometimes crossing "knee over knee." Men tend to keep their legs apart at a ten- to fifteen-degree angle, in a more open and relaxed stance.

12. Male body language is more likely to emphasize stature, composure, and confidence. Men also send signals of indifference, disagreement, or smugness far more often than women. Women are more likely to display enthusiasm and joy, and to visibly react when their feelings are hurt.

13. Women with breathy, tense voices are judged to be pretty, feminine, shallow, and unintelligent. Men with throaty, tense voices are thought to be mature, masculine, and intelligent.

The Anger Effect

Studies conducted at Yale and Northwest Universities found that women who have angry outbursts in professional settings are perceived as having less power, status, and competence than men who get angry. In fact, anger expressed by men often heightened their perceived status. But whether the woman was a CEO or a trainee, coworkers viewed any show of anger as a personal flaw; anger in men was seen as the result of external circumstances.[8]

LEADERSHIP STYLES OF MEN AND WOMEN

Generally speaking, women leaders tend to be more interactive, wanting to keep an encounter going until the emotional content has been played out. Women employ a more participative leadership style, they are more likely to share information and power and to foster collaborative environments, and they have strong relational skills that make them seem empathic to their staffs.

Whereas women focus on accommodating interpersonal needs, men don't place the same emphasis or value on the skills required to do so. Many men don't admire "people skills" as much as they do authority and control. Male leaders tend to be more transactional in their approach to business dealings, and once the transaction has been completed, they tend to move away from the interaction and back to solitary tasks. Men tend to favor a more hierarchical leadership style and to take a directive approach. Males are viewed as formal authorities and stronger leaders in roles that require more "command and control." This difference has appeared in both laboratory studies and observations of real leaders.

Obviously, both men and women lead successful teams, but even here I have observed differences. Male leaders tend to use competition—comparing team members' ideas—whereas women look for connections between team members' ideas. And here, once more, is a good argument for having both genders represented (and both collaborative processes valued) on a leadership team.

THE BODY LANGUAGE OF MALE AND FEMALE LEADERS

I recently conducted research with managers in the United States, Canada, and Europe about masculine and feminine communication styles and the problems and opportunities that the different styles create for leaders. I asked these four questions:

1. What is the greatest strength in male leaders' communication?

2. What is the greatest strength in female leaders' communication?

3. What is the greatest weakness in male leaders' communication?

4. What is the greatest weakness in female leaders' communication?

The responses indicated that both sexes identify the same set of strengths and weaknesses in themselves and each other. As you look at the findings that follow, notice how much of what people refer to as "communication" is determined or influenced by gender-specific nonverbal traits and behaviors.

Top Three Communication Strengths of Male Leaders

1. Physical presence

   "Men are bigger and look more powerful."

   "Men are more likely to have a formal office or executive title, which can make them seem (and feel) more authoritative."

2. Direct and forceful approach

   "Men get to the point when laying out the facts."

   "Men have deeper (more forceful) voices, they speak over you, and they dominate the conversation."

3. Body language signals of power and authority

   "Men keep a poker face that shows they can control their emotions."

   "Men have a confident 'power stance' and take up more room."

Top Three Communication Strengths of Female Leaders

1. Ability to read body language

   "Women have an ability to pick up on the subtle 'clues' of nonverbal communication."

   "Women have more insight into what's really going on."

2. Good listening skills

   "Women make more eye contact when someone else is talking."

   "Women are better at focusing attention on whoever is speaking."

3. Effective display of empathy

   "Women convey an aura of friendliness and welcome. This is more apparent in face-to-face communication because it is reflected in body language."

   "Women seem to be warmer—more approachable, expressive, and tuned in to others."

As you will see in the next set of responses, communication strengths turn into weaknesses when overdone.

Top Three Communication Weaknesses of Male Leaders

1. Overly blunt and direct

   "Men can be overbearing and loud."

   "Men are so blunt that it hurts people's feelings and dampens morale."

2. Insensitive to emotional reactions

   "Men can be too logical—and miss the heart or feelings behind the words."

   "Men don't listen. They don't even pretend to."

3. Too confident in own opinion

"Men interrupt all the time—as if their opinion is the only one that matters."

"They don't look as if they care about what people are saying."

Top Three Communication Weaknesses of Female Leaders

1. Overly emotional

"Women let their feelings show too much—and sometimes it looks as though they are losing control."

"I know many competent, experienced, and talented women who have cried in a business meeting—much to the dismay of themselves and the people they are meeting with."

2. Indecisive—won't get to the point

"Women will explain how to design a clock when I just want to know what time it is."

"Women can't look you in the eyes when delivering a tough message."

3. Lacking in authoritative body language signals

"Some women rely on girlishness or attractiveness to influence an outcome—instead of keeping the conversation on a professional level."

"Body language can be ambiguous or confusing due to using too many gestures."

BODY LANGUAGE TIPS FOR MALE AND FEMALE LEADERS

In the first chapter, I told you about two sets of signals that followers look for in their leaders: warmth (empathy, likeability, caring) and authority (power, credibility, status). Although I have coached many leaders of both sexes who do not fit the stereotypes, I've also observed that gender differences in body language most often do align with these two groupings. Women are usually the champions in warmth and empathy, but men display more power and authority cues.

Women send more warmth signals.

Men send more power signals.

If you are like most of the leaders I work with, there are situations in which your current nonverbal behavior is very effective—and other situations where you could benefit by having the flexibility to change the signals you are sending. (Often men's body language, instead of conveying confidence and competence, is perceived as cold and uncaring; women may undermine their authority by unknowingly using deference and submission signals.) Here are some tips on how to alter, accommodate, or modify your body language to be a more effective leader.

If you are a woman seeking to project authority and credibility,

• *Keep your voice down.* Women's voices often rise at the ends of sentences as if they're asking a question or asking for approval. When stating your opinion, use the authoritative arc, in which your voice starts on one note, rises in pitch through the sentence, and drops back down at the end.

• *Claim your space.* Females can compensate for men's larger and taller stature by standing straight, broadening their stance, spreading out their paperwork, and even putting their hands on their hips in order to take up more physical space. I've also advised women to stand when presenting their ideas, rather than staying seated at a conference table. This gives you a height and nonverbal status advantage.

• *Smile selectively.* Although smiling can be a powerful and positive nonverbal cue—especially for signaling likeability and friendliness—women should be aware that when excessive or inappropriate, smiling can also confuse people and compromise credibility—for example, if you smile out of context while discussing a serious subject, expressing anger, or giving negative feedback.

• *Watch your hands.* Everyone uses self-pacifying gestures when under stress. People rub their hands together, grab their upper arms, touch their necks, and so on. Because these can be distracting, their overuse by either sex lessens the appearance of authority and confidence. But, as a woman particularly, you will be viewed as much less powerful if you self-pacify with girlish behaviors (twirling hair, playing with jewelry, or biting a finger).

• *Curb your enthusiasm.* Women who express the entire spectrum of emotions often overwhelm their audience (especially if the audience is composed primarily of males). So in situations where you want to maximize your authority, minimize your movements. When you appear calm and contained, you look more powerful.

• *Speak up.* In negotiations, men talk more than women and interrupt more frequently. One perspective on the value of speaking up comes from former secretary of state Madeleine Albright, who—when asked what advice she had for up-and-coming professional women—replied, "Learn to interrupt."[9]

• *Straighten your head.* Head tilting is a positive signal that someone is interested and involved—and a particularly feminine gesture. But head tilting is also a universal sign of acquiescence and submission. When you want to project authority and confidence, you should hold your head in an erect, more neutral position.

• *Employ a firm handshake.* Even more than is the case for your male colleagues, your confidence and credibility will be judged by the firmness of your handshake. So review the handshake "rules" from Chapter Two and master a great grip.

• *Keep your eyes in the business zone.* As noted in Chapter Two, if you create an imaginary triangle with a base at eye level and an apex at mid-forehead, you will have mapped out the "business gaze." When you keep your focus in that area, you nonverbally signal a no-nonsense, businesslike approach. But when you move your focus from the eyes to the mouth, you turn your gaze into one that is more flirtatious and more appropriate for social encounters.

• *Dress like a leader.* I'm all for women dressing in a fashion that makes them feel attractive and confident, but I also advise women to take themselves (and their professional reputation) seriously. So "dressing for success" in a leadership role means dressing in ways that build, not diminish, your credibility. Women in managerial positions who dress in sexy attire (low-cut tops and too-short skirts) are viewed as less intelligent. Even other women take you less seriously.

Likeable Loser

Women gain likeability but lose the advantage in a negotiation when they flirt. In a UC Berkeley study, professors had female actors play the roles of sales representatives for a biotech business. Half were told to project a no-nonsense, businesslike approach. Half were instructed to flirt (using the nonverbal behaviors of smiling, leaning forward suggestively, tossing their hair, and so on)—but to do so subtly. The outcome was that the "buyers" offered the flirts 20 percent less, on average, than they offered the more straitlaced sellers. The only payoff for the flirts in the study was that they were deemed "more likeable."[10]

If you are a man seeking to project more warmth and empathy,

- *Try a little tenderness.* A man's ability to hold his emotions in check is viewed as an advantage in business negotiations. But that doesn't mean that men shouldn't allow their feelings to show in other business situations. Whether you are promoting collaboration, building employee enthusiasm for a new corporate direction, or addressing the negative consequences of a major change, showing emotion is not only a good thing: it is a powerful leadership strategy.

- *Look at people when they speak.* The amount of eye contact you give as a leader is especially telling if you reserve it only for those whose opinion you agree with. Women often cite a lack of eye contact as evidence that their male boss "doesn't value my input." So increasing your eye contact (and, most especially, making sure you are not looking at just some members of your team and ignoring others) will send signals of inclusiveness and warmth.

- *Stop solving problems.* Men's discomfort dealing with emotion (and their brain's innate response to it) leads them to immediately search for solutions, rather than understanding that sometimes people just need to be heard. The next time someone comes to you with an emotional problem, try being a sounding board rather than a problem solver.

- *Lighten up.* Men need to monitor their facial expressions, especially those that come across as intimidating, overpowering, or deliberately forbidding. Such visual power cues are certainly useful in some situations, but just as certainly not useful in others. The problem is, hard looks can become habitual in all your business dealings without your realizing it. You're the boss, so you scowl—period. Once you've become aware of that habit, however, you can begin to modify your facial expressions to suit the situation. An encouraging smile, for example, can go a long way if your goal is to build team morale and foster innovation. You'll still be the boss even if you do lighten up a bit, but when you do, you may be surprised to find your people responding with more positive contributions than you'd expected.

MEN ARE FROM MARS, WOMEN ARE FROM VENUS

Yes, as John Gray told us in his famous battle-of-the-sexes best seller twenty years ago, men and women are different—different in temperament, vision, understanding, intuition, analytical gifts, communication skills, emotional and creative strengths and weaknesses—plus a whole lot more ways too numerous to list here. Brain science explains many of these differences, as does the "behavioral molding" of upbringing and societal expectations. And there is much we are still learning.

Nothing about our experience of one another has changed since that book first appeared, nor will it in the future. A hundred years from now, men and women will still seem to have come from different planets. What has changed in business, however, is that the Venus-Mars dichotomy is beginning to make a critical impact on leadership philosophy and practice as more women lead teams, assume leadership roles, enter the (still) male-dominated upper echelons of corporations, and start their own businesses.

So I'm going to close this chapter with some useful words of advice about interplanetary cooperation: don't be afraid of aliens; they've come in peace, with the same aspirations as you have—to serve customers, build great products, help society, make money, work with friends, and create a brighter future.

7

WORKING WITH GLOBAL TEAMS

Body Language in a Multicultural World

On a speaking tour a few years ago, I traveled from the United Arab Emirates to China to India to Malaysia to the Philippines to Indonesia—and it seemed to me that in each country, the audience was arriving later and later. My speech in Jakarta was scheduled for 7:00 P.M. "Just ignore that announcement," I was advised. "We tell people to get here at seven, hoping they will arrive by eight. But just to be on the safe side, we never begin the program before nine."

Contrast that to a recent experience in Toronto, where my session was scheduled to open a conference at 8:00 A.M. In order to check the audiovisual equipment, I arrived an hour early, only to see a line of people already standing outside the auditorium. Concerned that I had misunderstood the agenda, I grabbed the meeting planner. "Don't worry," she assured me, "you've got plenty of time. We Canadians just have a habit of getting places early."

Here's the question: Which was right—the Indonesian concept of "rubber time" or the Canadian view of promptness?

Your answer, of course, depends on the cultural standards you are dealing with—because different cultures relate to time very differently. And the concept of time is only one of the nonverbal variants you will need to consider in order to work effectively with colleagues and associates whose cultural norms are different from your own.

Leadership today demands wide cultural acumen—not just because you have to participate increasingly in global teams, but also because the workforce within your own national borders is growing more diverse, ethnically and culturally. On any given business day, you can find yourself communicating face-to-face, over the phone, by e-mail, or by teleconference with people whose customs and cultures differ dramatically from your own.

This chapter and the next will help you communicate more effectively in a multicultural world by familiarizing you with the ways people from different cultures experience the world, and how those differences influence their nonverbal behavior in the business arena. We'll look at the distinction between so-called high- and low-context cultures, the important conceptual difference between time as a commodity and time as a constant, reserve versus effusion in the conduct of business, the subtle art of formal and informal behavior, why certain body language feels so right in one culture and so wrong—or even offensive—in another, and finally, which nonverbal signals are universal to all cultures.

CULTURE

In this chapter, the word *culture* refers primarily to a set of shared social values and assumptions that determine what is acceptable or "normal" behavior within a defined society (a nation, commonwealth, tribe, religious community, and so on). These values also serve a given society as a benchmark by which to judge the behavior of others. It is this second point you need to pay careful attention to when you're out there in the global arena. One little social blunder—an inappropriate remark, gesture, or expression—could cost you a contract, a vital introduction, or even an entire project. And without some basic understanding of the culture you're working in, you might not even know you've committed it!

Of course, you can't automatically presume that everyone you meet from a particular culture will exhibit identical nonverbal communication traits. Cultural stereotypes are valid only in that they provide clues about what to expect in general. Nor can you expect to fully understand all the layers and shades of meaning transmitted by nonverbal behavior in another culture. And you certainly can't view the behavior of others totally free of your own cultural bias—nor can others who are observing you. But you can adapt with reasonable success to almost any unfamiliar cultural environment by watching, listening, exercising a little patience and tolerance, and quietly modulating your own behavior in line with some of the basics that follow here.

High Context, Low Context

One very useful observational tool for dealing with an unfamiliar environment derives from a system of classification created by cultural anthropologist Edward T. Hall, which states that all cultures can be situated in relation to one another in terms of the styles in which they communicate. Low-context cultures (LCCs) communicate predominately through verbal statements and the written word. Low-context communication is explicit, direct, and precise, with little reliance on the unstated or implied. In high-context cultures (HCCs), communication depends more on sensitivity to nonverbal behaviors (body language, proximity, and the use of pauses and silence) and environmental cues, such as the relationship of the participants, what has occurred in the past, who is in attendance, and the time and place of the communication.[1]

Continuum of High-Context to Low-Context Cultures

High-Context Cultures

Japanese

Chinese

Arab

Greek

Mexican

Spanish

Italian

French

French Canadian

English

English Canadian

American

Scandinavian

German

German-Swiss

Low-Context Cultures

Source: L. Copeland and L. Griggs, 2001, *Going International: How to Make Friends and Deal Effectively in the Global Marketplace* (New York: Random House), p. 107.

Negotiators from LCCs tend to focus more on closing the deal, whereas those from HCCs are looking to build a relationship. When communicating across the "context divide" in global team meetings, LCC members might profit from taking extra time to get to know their HCC counterparts; HCC individuals might benefit from being more direct with LCC teammates, and understanding their need for "measurable progress." Everyone on the team could benefit from an open discussion and a deeper understanding of their cultural differences and similarities. The point, of course, isn't to abandon your cultural preferences but to increase cross-cultural effectiveness.

E-Mail from Japan

When I worked at a US-owned company, there was a team meeting. The marketing manager was the only American in attendance. The rest of the team (another marketing manager, engineers, designers, and manufacturers) came from Taiwan, France, Japan, Iran, and elsewhere. Most of us spoke very broken English, but the meeting was exciting and all were happy with the result—except the American. After the meeting he came to me and said "I'm the only guy who doesn't get it, so why don't you e-mail me a report?" All of us except for this one manager could understand each other through facial expressions, gestures and so on. Now that I think back, it seems like he relied too much on the verbal aspect of the communication.

—*Kazuhiro Amemiya, Japan*

Time—Commodity or Constant?

In the United States, we think of time as a linear commodity to "spend," "save," or "waste." Other cultures (including Italy, Brazil, and Japan) view time as a constant flow to be experienced in the moment, and as a force that cannot be contained or controlled. Whichever view you take can influence the way you conduct business.

When time is a commodity, adhering to a schedule becomes very important. I've seen the American fixation on timelines play right into the hands of negotiators from other cultures. A Japanese executive explained, "All we need to do is find out when you are scheduled to leave the country—and, by the way, it amuses us that you arrive with your return passage already booked—then we wait until right before your flight to present our offer. You are so anxious to stay on schedule, you'll give away the whole deal."

In cultures where the flow of time is a constant, it is viewed as a sort of circle in which the past, present, and future are all interrelated. In fact, in the Chinese languages there are no tenses to express past and future. Instead, "the three dimensions of time are always present and can be distinguished only through context."[2] Any important relationship is a durable bond that goes back and forward in time. In these cultures, relationships are pivotal to doing business, and it is often viewed as grossly disloyal not to favor friends and relatives in business dealings.

It's About Time

There's a joke about an American and a Chinese businessman sitting next to each other on a park bench in Hong Kong. The American says, "Well, you know I've been in Hong Kong for my company for thirty years. Thirty years! And in a few days they are sending me back to the States." The Chinese executive replies, "That's the problem with you Americans: here today and gone tomorrow."

Reserved or Effusive?

People from reserved cultures (like the Japanese, Chinese, Scandinavians, and Finns) tend to encourage speaking up only when there is something relevant to add to the conversation—and may have problems relating to people from cultures who constantly talk about seemingly irrelevant topics. Reserved cultures also tend to mask their feelings by keeping their emotional displays in check.

Effusive cultures encourage people to talk a lot as a means of indicating their warmth, passion, and interest. These cultures tend to interrupt more often and to avoid silence. They also tend to be more expressive and animated and to use larger and more frequent gestures. Examples of effusive cultures include the Arab countries, Italy, and Latin America.

If you're wondering how such an insignificant behavioral distinction could possibly have an impact on your organization's business decisions, consider the following:

An American-born Japanese IT manager requested a relocation to work at his company's Tokyo office. Excited about the possibility, he flew to Japan and interviewed with the local management team. His request was turned down. The reason? He was "too enthusiastic."

A Chinese-born, U.S.-educated, and highly qualified salesman was being considered for the job of sales manager for a new office in Shanghai. The American boss who conducted the interview decided that the salesman didn't demonstrate the "drive and aggression" needed to lead a sales department.

Of course, both evaluations may have been correct. But it is much more likely that the characteristics the interviewers wanted to see from the candidates were as much a reflection of their own respective cultures as an indicator of qualifications necessary for these jobs.

Formal and Informal

A U.S. executive in France made a conspicuous effort to socialize with lower-ranking staff members. His entirely logical intent was to boost morale, but his actions all but destroyed it. What the U.S. executive didn't know was that the French have a more structured and formal business culture, and that this kind of interlevel fraternizing is frowned on.

Should he have known this? Well, it would have helped his team-building efforts. Could he have known this? Yes, he could have—by being a little more observant and a little less sure of himself until he knew his business environment a little bit better. For a newcomer stepping into a formal arena like the French business culture, employing a small dash of reticence is always a good tactic in the beginning. Showing everybody what a great guy you are sometimes isn't such a great idea.

In informal cultures (like the United States, Canada, Australia, New Zealand, Denmark, Norway, and Iceland), people believe that inequality of social status or class should be minimized. The hierarchy in an organization is based more on differences in roles; individual ability and performance are most important. But in formal cultures (including European and Asian nations, the Arab world, the Mediterranean region, and Latin America), people are more likely to be treated with greater or less deference according to their social status, family background and connections, age, education, titles, degrees, and wealth.

In formal cultures, business protocol is highly valued, whereas it is seen as something inconvenient or tedious in informal cultures. People from informal cultures may regard their formal counterparts as distant, stuffy, pompous, or arrogant. People from formal cultures often find informality to be insulting. For example—and yes, I've seen all these behaviors in high-level global meetings over the years—if you slouch, chew gum, call people "pal" or "buddy" or by their first name on first acquaintance, cross your legs in an open-legged position, stretch out, or wear jeans and a tee shirt when everyone else is in a suit, you may be labeled "offensively informal." Or as one of my Malaysian clients explained with polite understatement, "We consider it rude and disrespectful to assume an intimacy that doesn't yet exist."

Assumptions you make about other cultures, even with the best of intentions, can also backfire if you haven't taken the time to verify them: "Once I attended a training session where the Canadian facilitator came dressed in flip-flops, long beads, and a white cotton breezy shirt. It was her first time in the Caribbean, and she made some terribly inaccurate assumptions about our culture. You see, everyone else in the room was dressed in a business suit" (Judette Coward-Puglisi, Trinidad and Tobago).

CROSS-CULTURAL BODY LANGUAGE

Some nonverbal signals are unique to a particular culture. Emblematic gestures fall into this category. For example, what we in the United States think of as a positive gesture, the "OK" sign with thumb and forefinger together creating a circle, has very different meanings in other cultures. In France it means "worthless" or "zero," in Japan it stands for money, and in other countries it represents a lewd or obscene comment.

There are, however, many nonverbal signals that cross cultural lines. In fact, body language that is controlled by the limbic brain (such as the freeze-fight-flight response to threat, blushing when embarrassed, and the need to self-pacify when under stress) can be seen around the world. We all use barriers—desks, crossed arms, turns to the side, hands clasped tightly—as methods of protection or making ourselves less vulnerable. And, although these may manifest differently, all cultures use gesture to add meaning to words, replace words, and (consciously or unconsciously) deliver unspoken information about the attitudes and feelings of the sender. One of these we've previously discussed is the "eyebrow flash," the universal body language cue that involves a sudden and quick raising of the eyebrows and widening of the eyes that occur when people encounter those they recognize and like.

Nonverbal communication is both instinctive (innate) and acquired (culturally determined). There are basic human emotions that are instinctive and universal, but their display is restricted by the "norms" of a particular culture—and the stimulus that triggers those emotions may also vary from culture to culture.

As we saw in Chapter One, scientists studied the aftermath of judo matches from the 2004 Olympic and Paralympic Games, comparing the behavior of winning and losing judo players. They found that victory looked the same (throwing their heads back, thrusting their arms in the air, puffing out their chests, and flashing big grins) across cultures. This was true even among athletes who were born blind and could never have learned the behavior from mimicking others.

There was a difference in the expression of shame, however. Among Western cultures, sighted athletes tended not to physically express shame—whereas their blind counterparts did. Researchers attributed this to the fact that shame is stigmatized in Western cultures, so repressing this emotion was a learned response.[3]

Universal Emotional Expressions

There is one area of body language that is identical in all cultures—the seven basic emotions that people around the world express, recognize, and relate to in the same way. Discovered and categorized by Paul Ekman and his colleagues at the University of California, San Francisco, the universal emotional expressions are joy, surprise, sadness, anger, fear, disgust, and contempt.[4] Here is how you can identify them:

Joy. The muscles of the cheeks rise, eyes narrow, lines appear at the corners of the eyes, and the corners of the mouth turn up.

Surprise. The eyebrows rise, and there is a slight raising of upper eyelids and dropping of the lower jaw.

Sadness. The eyelids droop as the inner corners of the brows rise and (in extreme sorrow) draw together, and the corners of the lips pull down.

Anger. The eyebrows are pulled together and lowered, the lower eyelid is tensed, the eyes glare, and the lips tighten, appearing thinner.

Fear. The eyebrows draw together and rise, the upper eyelid rises, the lower eyelid tenses, and the lips stretch horizontally.

Disgust. The nose wrinkles, the upper lip rises, and the corners of the mouth turn down.

Contempt. This is the only unilateral expression. The cheek muscles on one side of the face contract, and one corner of the mouth turns up.

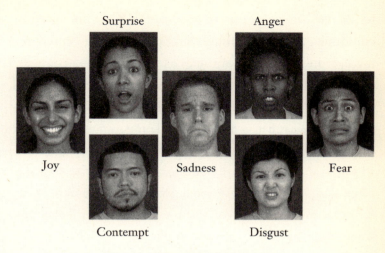

Surprise   Anger

Joy   Sadness   Fear

Contempt   Disgust

Universal emotional expressions

Whenever any of these emotions is felt strongly, its display is intense and can last up to four seconds. But, depending on a variety of influences (including an individual's cultural background), you may not see your team members exhibiting this stronger version. Emotional displays in corporate settings are often more subtle and fleeting.

Reading faces is a matter not just of identifying static expressions but also of noticing how faces subtly begin to change. (You do this every day without being aware of it. When you are in face-to-face exchanges, you watch the other person's changing expressions for all kinds of reactions and cues in order to gauge responses to what you just said.) Subtle expressions are emotions just starting to be shown, emotions experienced with a lower intensity, or emotions partially inhibited. Subtle versions of expressions involve the same facial muscles as their stronger counterparts, but are much less obvious. On more than one occasion, I've seen a slight expression of anger or disgust between colleagues, which has spoken volumes about the real underlying feelings between the two people. (I tend to watch the eyes. The small muscles around the eyes are often the site of real emotional giveaway—one part of the face that reacts before you even know how you feel about something that's been said or implied.)

Subtle expressions also contain a lot of useful information for managers and executives. David Matsumoto, founder of Humintell and a renowned expert in the field of nonverbal communication and emotions, has a "Subtle Expression Recognition Training" that was originally developed for government agencies. But I also recommend it to my leadership clients.[5] Leaders who develop their ability to decipher the not-so-obvious emotional reactions of team members gain a distinct advantage in establishing relationships, building rapport, eliciting information, and tracking how people really feel.

Micro expressions (lasting less than one-fifth of a second) are another way that an observer can get a glimpse into a person's true emotional state. But unless you are a trained expert (Humintell also provides training in this) or naturally gifted at spotting these fleeting visual impulses, they probably won't be helpful in a business setting. I'm not particularly adept at spotting micro expressions in real time, but I have "caught" several of them when analyzing people on videotape, when I could view an action repeatedly or slow it down.

Faked emotional reactions are more readily spotted. In general, expressions that are not genuine can be identified by the following behaviors:[6]

- A forced or faked expression does not use all the muscles in the face typically associated with that expression. One example previously mentioned is the smile that includes the mouth but does not involve the eye muscles.

- Because all real expressions (with the exception of contempt) are symmetrical, any other asymmetrical expression should be suspect.

- An expression that is of an unusually long duration (more than five seconds) is typically not genuinely felt. Most real expressions last only for a few seconds.

LESSONS LEARNED

I've learned a lot as I've observed global team meetings, and the most important lesson I can pass on to U.S. leaders is not to rush in with an American "take-charge attitude." In Hong Kong, I watched a newly arrived American executive meet with his Chinese team members—and destroy in five seconds the delicate relationship that the incumbent had taken over a year to build. Undoubtedly the new exec thought he was coming across as a hard-charging young businessman (which might have been the case back in the States), but in this culture, his actions were seen as rude, insensitive, and overbearing.

Like anyone else dealing with an international clientele, I have made my share of cultural faux pas. One particularly memorable one was when I started a global meeting with an "icebreaker" exercise—a tactic that we in the United States are particularly fond of. (After all, "time is money," so we need to find quick ways to get this "relationship-building stuff" in full swing.) I overheard a European participant say with a sigh, "Not another American icebreaker. Why don't they just wait until we thaw?"

I've also found that my international clients have been extremely generous in overlooking my cultural mishaps. As one client told me, "It will be fine, Carol. We know your heart is in the right place." Aretha Franklin was right—it all starts with R-E-S-P-E-C-T. If you show a genuine respect for other cultures' norms and values, and if your heart's in the right place—even if you make an occasional blunder—it will be fine.

8

INTERNATIONAL BODY LANGUAGE

Input from Twelve Experts

I have worked (given speeches or seminars, coached or consulted) in twenty-four countries, and I have traveled to a dozen more. But I certainly don't consider myself an expert on international business practices. I do, however, have access to a network of businesspeople who are experts—professionals and communicators from around the world, many of whom are affiliated with the International Association of Business Communicators (IABC). This chapter is a compilation of their insights and experiences with global body language and business protocol. In this chapter, you'll get a multicultural perspective of how eye contact, touch, space, emotional expression, and greeting behaviors are exhibited in a business meeting; you'll increase your ability to understand and identify cultural differences; and you'll be able to anticipate more accurately how your behavior is likely to be perceived.

I'd like to introduce my panel of experts....

Marc Wright (United Kingdom) is the publisher of www.simply-communicate.com, the online resource and magazine used by fifteen thousand internal communication professionals around the world. Marc is chair of IABC Europe & Middle East; chair of simplyexperience, an event and video production company; and chair of simplygoodadvice, a consultancy specializing in internal communication.

Paulo Soares (Brazil) is a professional with broad experience in business communication. He currently works as corporate communications general manager of Vale (a multinational mining company), responsible for the communication in Brazil. He also serves on the IABC international board and is a member of the ABERJE (the Brazilian association of business communication).

Helen Wang (China) is originally from China, but has lived in the United States for over twenty years. After receiving her master's degree from Stanford University, Helen worked in a think tank and consulted for Fortune 500 companies. Helen is also an entrepreneur in Silicon Valley and has worked extensively with business communities in China. Author of *The Chinese Dream: The Rise of the World's Largest Middle Class*, Helen advises and consults for companies doing business in China.

Judette Coward-Puglisi (Trinidad and Tobago) is the managing director of Mango Media Caribbean, a strategic communications firm serving global clients. Judette is a former award-winning documentary producer and journalist and the founding president of IABC Trinidad and Tobago.

Jennifer Frahm (Australia) is the director of her own change management and communication consultancy, Jennifer Frahm Collaborations, in Melbourne. She is the founder of Conversations of Change, an off-site retreat for people wanting to make change in their businesses and careers. She is the current chapter president of IABC Victoria, Australia.

Roberto Islas (Mexico) is the director of international private banking for HSBC Private Bank (UK) Ltd. A native Mexican, Roberto has an extensive knowledge of the Latin American markets.

Silvia Cambié (Germany) speaks five languages and has spent her entire career in an international environment. She is a business communicator and journalist, currently based in London, where she runs Chanda Communications and advises clients on strategic communication, stakeholder relations, and social media. Silvia serves as a director on the executive board of IABC and is the coauthor of *International Communications Strategy: Developments in Cross-Cultural Communication, PR and Social Media.*

Priya Sarma (United Arab Emirates) has worked with the leading advertising agencies in both India and Egypt. Currently she is the corporate communication manager for Unilever, leading the function across North Africa Middle East as well as Central Africa. She is based in Dubai.

Kazuhiro Amemiya (Japan) worked as a corporate communication manager and a webmaster at Texas Instruments Japan and Intel Japan, before establishing Crossmedia Communications, Inc. Kaz has helped communication managers and webmasters strategize their online communication ever since. He is a member of IABC and the Public Relations Society of Japan.

Sujit Patil (India) has close to fourteen years of experience across all the facets of business communication—marketing communications, branding, PR, crisis communications, and internal communications. He leads a comprehensive communications function at Tata Chemicals Ltd., a leading chemicals company with manufacturing operations across Asia, Europe, Africa, and the United States. He won the 2010 IABC Gold Quill Excellence award for employee communications.

Saada Ibrahim Mufuruki (Tanzania) is the managing director of M&M Communications Ltd., one of the leading communications agencies in Tanzania. Saada started her communications career with Ogilvy & Mather and later joined ScanAd Kenya. In 1992, she was appointed CEO of ScanAd Tanzania. Saada is the vice chair of the

Advertising Practitioners Association of Tanzania and is the Tanzania chapter president of IABC.

Laine Santana (the Philippines) is the senior corporate communications manager for HSBC Asia-Pacific, covering news management and investor relations messaging for the region. She set up the public affairs department in HSBC, and as vice president was instrumental in building the bank's profile and reputation as it expanded its business in the Philippines.

I asked each of the panelists to help me coach a (fictitious) senior manager from the United States in the nonverbal and cross-cultural aspects of attending a business meeting in his or her respective country. Here are the eight questions I asked:

1. How do you greet business partners?

2. How do you exchange business cards?

3. What does it mean to be "on time" for a meeting?

4. How close do you stand in a conversation with a business colleague, and how often do you touch?

5. What amount of eye contact is appropriate between businesspeople?

6. If the meeting were around a conference table, where would your most senior executive sit, and where would the American executive be seated?

7. What is the role of emotion in business dealings?

8.   Would any of this advice be different if the U.S. executive were a woman?

GREETING BEHAVIORS

The handshake is fast becoming a universal business greeting, but there are still some very interesting cultural variations. The Japanese give a light handshake. Germans offer a firmer shake with one pump, and the French grip is light with a quick pump. Middle Eastern people will continue shaking your hand throughout the greeting. And don't be surprised if you are occasionally met with a kiss, a hug, or a bow somewhere along the way. Here is what the panelists said:

Marc (UK): When shaking hands, dominant males will try to angle their wrist to make their hand uppermost. Women often drop their gaze during a handshake and will tend to disengage first. Kissing is becoming more in evidence, but more prevalent between women. Men will only kiss a woman if they know them well. Men very rarely hug each other—and never ever kiss each other.

Paulo (Brazil): It will depend on how formal the business is and if you have met the people before. Shaking hands is the most common, but one or two kisses (depending on what region of Brazil you are in) can happen between male and female. Hugs will happen if you have any intimacy with your business partners. That can happen between males, females (more common), and also males and females.

Jennifer (Australia): In Australia, it is customary and appropriate to greet with a firm handshake whether you are male or female. If you are a female and you receive a soft or limp handshake from a male, it usually signifies a male executive who has not come to terms with women in the workplace and thinks that you may need "special" treatment.

Roberto (Mexico): In Mexico, you greet mainly with a handshake if it's the first time you meet the prospect-client-partner. Thereafter it is not uncommon to kiss once (the ladies) and hug the men. Latin Americans are kind of expected to do this, after two or three meetings; people from Anglo countries tend to take longer to hug, and this is understood. If it is a well-known business partner, you would always kiss (ladies) or hug (men).

Silvia (Germany): Germany has a very formal business culture. Shaking hands is the expected greeting. And it is very important that your grip is firm and "determined." People will evaluate you from it. A kiss on the cheek is rare, but maybe a bit more common in southern Germany, or between businesswomen (or former colleagues) if they know each other well.

Priya (UAE): Locals greet each other with a hug and three kisses on the cheeks. This holds for both men and women. In Arabia (Gulf and the Kingdom of Saudi Arabia

[KSA]), between men the traditional greeting is one rub of the nose. When local men greet local women, they both bow slightly at the waist and put their hand on the left side of their chest (over the heart). However, with an increasingly large number of expatriates in the Middle East, when locals meet foreigners or expatriates, they shake hands. In KSA, though, men and women (even when meeting expats) never shake hands.

Kaz (Japan): If both parties are Japanese, people make a light bow, even if one person works at a foreign-affiliated company or deals with foreigners on a daily basis. When we greet a foreigner, we usually shake hands. Kissing or hugging hardly ever, if not never, occurs among Japanese in a business setting, but those styles of greeting appear to be more acceptable if the other person is a foreigner and both have known each other very well.

Sujit (India): A confident handshake is a preferred first contact. The "duration" of the handshake is a tricky situation. A major discomfort is a handshake that lasts the entire introduction! For me, a quick, firm, warm, and nondomineering yet engaging handshake works the best. The vibes should be good and accompanied by an empathetic smile rather than a cocky, materialist one. Although men rarely hug on the first meeting, for associates who have been in contact for long but have never met before, side hugs work well in demonstrating affection, warmth, and the fact that the person was looking forward to the meeting.

Saada (Tanzania): It depends on the situation as follows. In business meetings, if it is man-to-man or woman-to-man, it would be a handshake. The males normally continue the handshake long after the greetings. The handshake is normally strong between the men. Depending on the seniority, age, or position, the junior person would have his left hand holding his or her wrist during the handshake as a sign of respect. (One note: If it is a greeting among staunch Muslims, a man will not shake hands with or kiss a woman if she is not his sister, mother, grandma, or aunt. Greeting is purely verbal.)

If the greeting is between ladies and they know each other, then it would be a kiss on both cheeks with no handshakes. If they are meeting for the first time or have met just a couple of times, they will just shake hands.

Laine (Philippines): In the Philippines, a firm handshake is still the most appropriate for both men and women. Eye contact is important to establish rapport and focus, and a smile is a plus that will surely put both parties at ease. For colleagues (men with women or women with women) who have known each other for some time, it is becoming common to greet each other with a kiss. Here it's a one-cheek (air) kiss. Sometimes it doesn't happen upon introduction, but after warming up with a first meeting, they say good-bye with a buss. For men, a handshake at the start and end of a meeting will suffice.

BUSINESS CARDS

In the United States, we are very casual with business cards—handing them out as a poker player might deal a deck of playing cards. As you can see from the panelists' comments, other cultures have different (and sometimes ritualistic) ways of exchanging business cards.

Marc (UK): Many Brits don't have or use them, as we expect people to trust us—"our word is our bond." When people hand out business cards, there is usually a flurry with a pen as they adjust their latest title, e-mail address, or mobile number with the phrase, "I've been meaning to update these for ages."

Paulo (Brazil): After exchanging the cards, we usually put them on the table where we have the meeting in order to keep the people's names in mind.

Helen (China): The Chinese hand out business cards with both hands. Sometimes they even bow a little while holding the business cards above their heads to show respect. When you receive someone else's business card, always look at it and acknowledge it. When you put it away, place it carefully in your card case or with your business documents.

Judette (Trinidad and Tobago): In a formal meeting, we wait for the senior person to take out his or her business card. We tend to be polite and show interest by actually looking at the card.

Jennifer (Australia): The giving and receiving of business cards is reserved for relationships that matter in Australia. We view those who hand out business cards indiscriminately as not to be trusted and probably trying to sell something. If you are told, "Oh, I don't have my new card; they are still at the printers," you may have made the Australian nervous, and he or she is planning an immediate exit.

Roberto (Mexico): Usually you give them out with the handshake. People look at them, and if it's a formal meeting, you keep them on the top of the table. If it is in a restaurant, you put them in your pocket.

Silvia (Germany): Business cards hold a great importance—especially at the beginning of a meeting. Germans will check it to see your title and level within your company. At one meeting, an Italian executive didn't have a business card (which is quite common in that culture), and my German colleagues couldn't believe it.

Priya (UAE): They are handed out formally at the start of the meeting as a form of introduction. There is no ceremony or process to their handing out.

Kaz (Japan): Exchanging business cards is considered *the* most important part of greeting. (Freshmen even learn the appropriate way—like a ritual.) It has to be very polite. We are expected to give and receive business cards with both hands and with a light bow. Be sure to present your card so that the other person does not have to turn it over to read your information.

Sujit (India): Like most Indians, I would take it as an insult if someone just took my card and put it in his pocket without even reading it! On a very formal first meeting, many professionals use both hands while giving and receiving the cards and also reflexively bow a bit. Designations and hierarchies matter in corporate India, and it is always good to take a few seconds to read the card and maybe acknowledge it before you stack them in the purse or a pocket. I always appreciate a person who writes down on the back of my card the context, reference, date of meeting, and so on. The nonverbal communication I get in this action is that he or she is interested in getting back in contact.

Saada (Tanzania): Mostly the card is passed around the table, or one goes round the table and hands out a card to each person.

Laine (Philippines): In the Philippines, we usually present the card with both hands to the recipient. The receiver will acknowledge with thanks and a nod and take some time to look at the card details before keeping it or laying it on the table for easy reference, especially if meeting a number of people.

TIME

Whether time is perceived as a commodity or a constant determines the meaning and value of being "on time." Misunderstandings can occur when one culture views arriving late for a meeting as bad planning or a sign of disrespect, while another culture views an insistence on timeliness as childish impatience. If a meeting is scheduled to start at 2 P.M. and end at 4 P.M., when would you show up? And when would you expect to be finished? Simple questions, but with culturally determined answers.

Marc (UK): Up to 2:08 start time is acceptable; 2:15 is considered rude. Could overrun to 4:15. Attendees will mostly be attentive, but it is acceptable to be suddenly called out. Around half will have laptops open. All will do BlackBerry checks from time to time. Everyone stops for tea, which has a quasi religious dimension in UK meetings. Quality of biscuits (cookies) will be remarked upon.

Paulo (Brazil): Brazilians are not very "on time" for their meetings and events. Up to thirty minutes late is okay, and meetings usually are not scheduled to finish on time. There is a time for them to start, but never to finish.

Helen (China): Some Chinese do not take it seriously to be on time for a meeting, although this is changing. The Chinese tend to have spontaneous meetings. It is very hard to schedule a meeting ahead of time. They do not keep a calendar. Once, I tried to schedule a meeting with a Chinese colleague two days prior; he said, "Call me the day you want to meet, and we can make an arrangement." It's acceptable that people show up to meetings fifteen to twenty minutes late.

Judette (Trinidad and Tobago): Assume the meeting will begin at 2 P.M. and be there for 2; be prepared to indulge in light chatting about sports, social events on the national calendar, and so on before diving into the meeting. Assume the meeting won't end at 4 P.M. and leave yourself some flexibility.

Jennifer (Australia): The meeting should start at 2 P.M., and anything later than ten minutes past is considered bad manners. Likewise we expect the meeting to finish on time. In corporate environments, the day is dominated by meetings, so when one runs late, so do the others. The exception is the Very Important Person, who will communicate his or her importance by running late from other Very Important Meetings.

Roberto (Mexico): This is a very complex issue. In Mexico, people are almost always "fashionably late" (up to half an hour). If you are meeting a client, you are expected to be on time; the client can always be late, and it is not uncommon. Also, it is rare to put "end times" to meetings; they usually go until finished. As they usually start late, putting an end time would not work, and may actually be seen as pressure, which is negative.

Silvia (Germany): It is very important to be punctual—and to keep the agenda, coffee breaks, and so on, on time. So if we say the meeting is 2 to 4 P.M., people will arrive at 1:50 and expect to leave promptly at 4. If you don't adhere to a strict schedule and if you don't end as scheduled (or at least have an apology and a logical explanation for why you aren't doing so), you will be judged as "sloppy," and your professionalism will be questioned.

For a business meeting, you need to show that you are prepared. You must have a written agenda. Everything needs to be itemized—and distributed in advance, if possible. The person chairing the meeting will introduce everyone (name, title, position in company), and either explain why each person is attending or ask the individuals to do so.

In German there is a word (Nachbereitung) that roughly translates as "preparation for the follow-up." So, after the meeting, it is common to send another document with a "thank you" for attending the productive meeting and a short list of conclusions reached at the meeting.

Priya (UAE): In the Middle East, relationships rather than time are the focus. Also, given the busy roads and so on, meetings are expected to start late. So one always provides for a delayed start and ending. Because of the focus on relationships, to be the most effective in the Middle East, expect the first five minutes of a business meeting conversation to be dominated by personal talk during which families and other informal topics are asked about. It is considered rude to immediately jump into a business conversation.

Kaz (Japan): If the meeting is supposed to start at 2 P.M., it is acceptable until 2:10. A person at a higher position—a manager or a team leader, for example—may show up fifteen to thirty minutes late and no one would blame.

As I worked at a foreign (U.S.-based) company, I noticed that meetings would be done on time if not earlier. In comparison, meetings with Japanese companies fully occupied the scheduled time and in worst cases went on more than an hour longer. (Japanese companies seem to care more about beginning on time than wrapping up on time.)

Sujit (India): There is a joke that runs in India. It is called the IST, Indian Standard Time, that is generally off the actual time by over twenty minutes or so ... sometimes even more! It is always good and expected that there is an agenda with timelines, else you may run a danger of huge delays. Generally meetings start on time, a small delay of a few minutes is not even considered, and delays of close to fifteen minutes are considered normal. The situation is changing, though, and more often than not, meetings begin on time. My experience has been that as compared to American or British professionals, Indians are pretty verbose, and that adds to the time factor. It is always recommended that there is a small cushion on the timelines to accommodate delays.

Indian professionals are known for multitasking, and one should not be surprised that a lot of going out and coming in happens during a meeting. This should not be considered insulting. With multitasking and multiple tasks handled simultaneously, checking mails or taking calls on BlackBerrys or cell phones, though not considered polite, is a normal trend and is generally accepted.

Generally, meetings are laced with snacks, tea or coffee, and so on, which is considered as a hospitality ritual.

Saada (Tanzania): To be on time means being there either five minutes before or exactly on time. Anything

210

later will show the person lacks seriousness and is not professional. Meetings at times could get delayed if most members are late, so the start time could be 2:00 or 2:15. End time could be 4:15 or later depending on how strict the chairperson is with time.

Meetings here are extremely formal, and the person in charge of the agenda is the one who is conducting the meeting. In every meeting you will find tea, coffee, and biscuits. If meetings run into lunch, then there is a light snack. Mobile phones are usually switched off or put on silent. Texting or stepping out to take a call comes across as being rude.

Laine (Philippines): In the Philippines, people are more tolerant about timing in general, especially in local offices. In some cases, like government offices, expect to wait longer. (Hopefully this is changing!) But if you're meeting an executive of a large corporate firm or a multi-national, he or she is likely to be more time conscious. In any case, it is still advisable to always be on time. Traffic in cities like Manila can be quite troublesome, so allow some extra time to get to your meetings and plan your route in advance.

DISTANCE AND TOUCH

When it comes to distance and touch, people's comfort levels differ measurably across cultures. Some cultures formally distance themselves from one another when doing business, getting close only to shake hands or exchange business cards. Other cultures conduct business at a much closer interpersonal distance and use a greater frequency of touch cues.

Marc (UK): Brits stand at least two feet apart—and hardly ever touch business colleagues. Sometimes they might tap the table with a pen close to the person they are connecting with, but bodily contact is avoided.

Paulo (Brazil): Distance isn't an issue for us. We can sit close or even stand very close to our business colleagues. Hugging and touching are quite common in Brazil—especially in comparison with other cultures.

Helen (China): The Chinese tend to stand close in a conversation, less than two feet, but more than one foot. Sometimes they touch the other person's arm or back or grasp a shoulder to show that they have established a trusting relationship. The Chinese may also bump into you while walking or talking. It's not considered rude in Chinese culture to bump into other people.

Judette (Trinidad and Tobago): Certainly men will not touch much, if at all; a pat on the shoulder at the end of a good meeting may be all. We stand about two feet apart.

Jennifer (Australia): Although known for their relaxed and easygoing countenance, Australians are surprisingly uptight about distance. If you stand closer than two feet, it is considered intense and possibly an indication that you are to be told something very confidential. Unless there was a preexisting close relationship, an Australian would take a step backwards or sideways to create space. We are more comfortable with three to four feet apart.

Australians would flinch or stiffen at a touch from a business colleague. Most male executives would be concerned about the legal implications of touching a female in the workplace. If there is a light touch on the arm or shoulder, it communicates "I am like you; I am one of you," or "I appreciate what you have done."

Roberto (Mexico): You stand close and constantly touch. If you don't know the other person well, you would touch mainly the arm, shoulder, and back. If you know the person well, sometimes you lightly touch the leg if you are sitting next to each other.

Silvia (Germany): Germans are more comfortable when keeping a good arm's distance away. And you won't see much touching, but it is more common in southern Germany.

Priya (UAE): Here people stand close, as the concept of personal space does not exist; instead it is about proximity, as all transactions are dominated by relationships. In fact, if people stand too far apart, it is seen as a negative, and you can be asked why you are standing at a distance. However, not much touching happens in deference to the laws of the land where members of the opposite sex not related to each other by marriage are not supposed to touch each other in public.

Kaz (Japan): We prefer to be three to four feet apart. Two feet makes us feel almost uncomfortable. (A close physical proximity is unexpected except for the rush-hour trains, literally packed with passengers, where we simply give up and accept the situation.) In Japan, people hardly ever touch their business colleagues, especially these days. Sometimes male managers pat their male colleagues' shoulders for encouragement.

Sujit (India): About two feet is a good distance. However, sometimes I have experienced senior professionals coming too close and almost whispering; it could be their style, but it generally puts people off! It is generally good to have a decent distance during conversations, a demeanor that is respectful, and a body language that is open (no folded arms close to the chest!). Shorter distances are okay on an evening out and over drinks. Moreover, when it comes to ladies, sufficient care needs to be taken on how close one wants to stand and talk.

Generally in a business scenario, the only touch that happens is the handshake on meeting and parting. Indians are generally warm, and an innocuous pat to congratulate or asking someone to stop is not seen as offensive. An innocent touch on the arm and shoulder to reassure someone is a normal behavior. A high-five among peers during a meeting is also a way of showcasing solidarity.

Saada (Tanzania): At least a foot apart. I normally would touch or tap on the wrist or shoulder, but very lightly.

Laine (Philippines): Two feet should be a good estimate for the Philippines, regardless of gender. For women, more senior executives would tend to be more formal and conscious of propriety. Touching is usually not appropriate among business colleagues, especially if in a meeting context. Maybe during cocktails, or in a more casual atmosphere, a light tap on the arm or shoulder, especially among colleagues who know each other well, is acceptable.

EYE CONTACT

The rules of eye contact vary from culture to culture. In the United States (and other countries), people are taught to look at each other during conversations, but in some cultures, minimizing eye contact is considered a sign of respect.

Marc (UK): Brits use a reasonable amount of eye contact, but there's much looking into the air when discussing controversial issues.

Paulo (Brazil): Eye contact is common and shows how confident you are about an issue.

Helen (China): The Chinese tend to avoid eye contact. It's considered impolite if you look straight in the eyes of the other person. The Chinese can be very uncomfortable with eye contact.

Judette (Trinidad and Tobago): We like eye contact, but there's a fine line between men and women. If a man, don't take the woman's warmth and friendliness as a sign that the lady is interested in you—particularly at a Carnival party! They're just enjoying themselves. If a woman, aim for courtesy and warm interest, but be careful about sending mixed messages.

Jennifer (Australia): Australians hold eye contact to denote trustworthiness and respect. Someone who does not look at you is probably telling fibs or doesn't think highly of you. Someone who holds prolonged eye contact without polite breaks will make others uncomfortable. Prolonged eye contact can be used as a deliberate tactic to unsettle the other business partner.

Roberto (Mexico): Always look at someone in the eyes.

Silvia (Germany): Eye contact is necessary. You won't be trusted without it.

Priya (UAE): A reasonable amount of eye contact is expected to actually make any sort of an impact. However, staring is considered rude.

Kaz (Japan): Only the leader of the business meeting or the speaker will make a reasonable amount of eye contact, but if a participant makes just as much eye contact, it may be interpreted as rejecting the idea or having something to say against it. In other words, a minimum amount of eye contact is appropriate in Japan between businesspeople.

Sujit (India): I would personally like to believe that Indians operate more on the trust factor, and one of the key essentials to generate trust is empathetic eye contact during a conversation. It also depicts confidence. Although eye contact is important, unnecessary staring is considered discourteous, especially if one is looking too long at a lady participant.

Saada (Tanzania): Too much eye contact could be seen as domineering. It also depends on the sex: male to male, if it is prolonged a little, could be seen as okay, but male to female could be seen as being aggressive or overconfident.

Laine (Philippines): Eye contact is very important to show engagement and sincerity. In the Philippines, though, you may still encounter those who remain quite self-conscious when looking people in the eye or maintaining eye contact. You will find that some may still tend to look away or down on occasions. But this is less true now, especially among the younger executives.

SEATING

You are the guest—so where will you be seated at the conference table? And where will your host sit? It all depends....

Marc (UK): Senior execs always sit at the head of table. Any U.S. members will tend to sit in the middle and upset the hierarchy of above- and below-the-salt protocols. This goes back to medieval times when salt was a luxury and the nobility would always sit at or above the salt, whereas more lowly types would gravitate toward the bottom half of the table.

Paulo (Brazil): The most important senior executive usually sits at the head of the table or in the middle. His or her assistants can sit next to him (on the right and left). We would seat an American executive across from our senior executive or on his right.

Helen (China): The most senior Chinese executive would sit where he or she could face the door across the table. The Chinese believe that position gives the person a lot of power and control. The American executive would be seated next to the most senior executive.

Judette (Trinidad and Tobago): Wait for the most senior persons to sit; business partners normally sit opposite.

Jennifer (Australia): We're very free-form in seating at conference tables. There is usually some discussion of "Where do you want me to sit?" but unless it is a very formal meeting, the most senior executive sits at the seat that is left for him or her (as this person is usually late) owing to the fact he or she is a Very Important Person. The person running the meeting sits at the head of the table usually. He or she may also choose to sit at the middle of the table so as to be seen to be inclusive of others and not hierarchical.

Roberto (Mexico): The most senior always sits at the head of the table.

Silvia (Germany): The German executive will sit at the head of the table or in the middle of one of the sides. If he is at the head, he will probably want an aide to be seated next to him. The American exec will be seated at one of the sides—across from the exec if he's in the middle—or down the table if he's at the end.

Priya (UAE): The most senior head would sit at the head of the table, and he would lead the discussion.

Kaz (Japan): In Japan, the guests take seats at the far side of the table from the entrance door. At each side of the table, the most senior executive sits in the middle, a person second in the hierarchical order takes the far end of the table, and staff sit closest to the door.

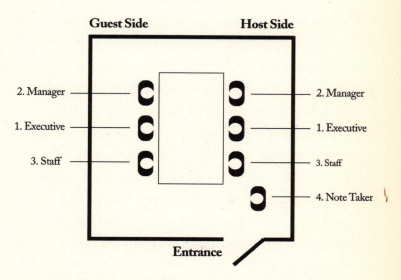

Seating arrangements for a Japanese business meeting

Sujit (India): While the most senior executive occupies the narrow end of the conference table (the head position), I feel it depends on the situation and the type of meeting. Generally this position is reserved for the senior-most people for any general organizational meeting.

For a conference table meeting, two scenarios come to my mind:

1. *A negotiation when the American is a supplier to the Indian buyer.* The instinctive position that the buyer would take would be the center of one side of the table, flanked by his or her team. The supplier and that team would occupy the space across to have a face-to-face meeting. Generally the buyer team would be larger than the supplier team. This is also to convey in a nonverbal way a commanding position in one's own sphere of influence.

2. *A general sales pitch.* This is a situation when spontaneously the most senior executive would take the head position. This is the position that has the best view of all participants. The presenters would be in a row perpendicular and at the other end to operate and present on the screen facing the head position. (While the senior-most person gets to see the screen straight, the others generally have to turn their necks right or left depending on the side of the table occupied!) The nonverbal cue here is that the person occupying the head position is in control and has to grasp the situation correctly, as he is the one responsible for the final decision.

Saada (Tanzania): The person who is chairing the meeting sits at the head of the table, and his or her team would be beside him or her. The visitors would sit on the opposite side. This is a typical setup for external meetings. For internal meetings, the person chairing the meeting sits at the head, the management team next to him or her, and the other invited team members on the opposite side.

Laine (Philippines): Senior executives tend to take the head of the table. The guest would most likely take his or her cue from the host. The host may point to the seat as he or she invites the guest to sit down. It is still safe to sit across if the table is small; sitting beside each other has become acceptable. If the guest is conscious of proximity, he or she can skip one seat.

EMOTIONS

The display of emotions allowed (even expected) in a business meeting differs greatly from culture to culture. What will be the reaction if you laugh out loud, rant and rave about some negotiation point, disclose personal information, or burst into tears? Here's what the panel had to say.

Marc (UK): Emotion is allowed more than in Nordic countries, whom we consider to be a bit buttoned up. Jokes are preferred to raw emotion, and sarcasm and irony are much valued. Passion is limited unless the subject of sport comes up. To shout is an admission of defeat, and although laughter is encouraged, tears are a source of major embarrassment. Coolness and aloof detachment are valued. Anything else is described as "losing it."

Paulo (Brazil): We are very emotional. We usually start a meeting talking about our families, friends, personal lives, and so on, and after a warm-up, we get into business. Examples and personal information are often used during meetings.

Helen (China): The Chinese can get emotional in business meetings, including laughing, or raising their voices. Talking loud is not considered rude.

Judette (Trinidad and Tobago): The T&T private sector tends to be less formal than other parts of the Caribbean. Our culture is jovial, and on many occasions a joking and jesting atmosphere is the preferred way to start a meeting. Crying may be perceived as irrational.

Jennifer (Australia): Australians prefer business dealings to be emotionally neutral. Anger, distress, and excessive emotion will make an Australian uncomfortable in the workplace. Most emotion in the workplace is perceived as career limiting.

Roberto (Mexico): Emotion is part of Mexican people. It will always be shown. There's usually a bit of comedy if the air gets tense, and a lot of banter.

Silvia (Germany): Some emotions are acceptable. You should expect to see displays of power and even rage (raised voice, accusatory tone, emphatic speech).

It's a normal negotiation tactic to begin with an attack. What they are looking for is your reaction. If you are cowed, they will tend to dismiss you. If you respond with confident and powerful body language, you will be respected.

Priya (UAE): This is a part of the world where emotions and relationships dominate transactions. So people do get emotional and show their displeasure. However, in certain places like Dubai, extreme aggression and even calling people names can land you in jail.

Kaz (Japan): Traditionally it is not encouraged to show emotions, as Japan has long cherished a high-context culture, and people have been expected to "sense" what the others mean without explicit emotional expressions. Yet as Japan shifts to a low-context society, emotional expressions are more encouraged than before. Another aspect of emotional expression in Japan is that people follow the expressions of others, such as laughter, simply to "do the same." For instance, even if we do not understand or appreciate the joke, we reciprocate the laughter or a smile as good manners if other people laugh.

Sujit (India): Although Indians are emotional, not many would show this side in a business dealing. Laughter and lighter moments are always accepted well and act as stress busters. A demonstration of concern, empathy, and cohesion helps gather trust faster. But sarcastic, racist, and domineering emotions get easily manifested in conversations and body language, and these are a big put-off during a business meeting or any other meeting.

Saada (Tanzania): One is expected to be calm and cool throughout the meeting. If you are angry, you are supposed to show it through your facial expression and tone of voice, but not to shout or scream. Foul or loose language is not accepted and is seen as demeaning. Breaking down in tears for a woman is seen as a sign of weakness, and for a man it is unacceptable. It also comes across as being unprofessional. Jokes are seen as okay as long as they are light ones. It is seen as okay to laugh at a joke, but not when one is trying to say or express something.

Laine (Philippines): It is best to respond or act with a degree of restraint and propriety. You can smile or laugh when the situation calls for it—and in a culture of happy people, this is more a norm than an exception. Shouting or emotional outbursts are not recommended even if these acts are just forms of expression and not intentionally meant to embarrass. Diplomacy in word and action is encouraged. It is also advisable to express emotions one-on-one rather than in front of the whole group, especially if not everyone is involved in the situation. Filipinos find it difficult to detach an issue or discussion from the person. They tend to get affected by an open confrontation, or sometimes by an opposing idea or comment. Generally, they are very sensitive.

WOMEN

Many of the panelists said that their advice would be the same if I were coaching a female executive for a meeting in their cultures. A typical comment was, "Women are viewed as business counterparts and are treated (and expected to behave) similarly to men in senior executive roles." There were, however, some exceptions:

Marc (UK): Men never offer to make refreshments, and they expect others to pour the tea. If there is one woman among a dozen men, no one will pour tea unless she takes on the responsibility. We have the phrase in all-male meetings: "Who will be mother?"

Helen (China): Chinese men may compliment women's appearance, such as by using the word "attractive" or "pretty." Some language may sound inappropriate in American culture, but they are just trying to be friendly.

Roberto (Mexico): Mexico is mainly a male-driven country. Things are changing, but how people act definitely changes if there is a woman present. If a group is made up of only men, usually the banter can get elevated, particularly if they are all peers; if there is one or more senior men, the setting is more formal. If there is a woman, this is also the case, unless she is well known to everyone, at which stage everyone relaxes more.

Silvia (Germany): People outside Germany believe that the country is rather advanced in workplace gender issues, but this is not really the case. Women in senior leadership positions are still rare. My best advice for visiting women executives is to stay very business focused. Tone down feminine flirtatious behavior. Instead, project confidence and power, and you'll be fine.

Sujit (India): Women executives certainly have an advantage. Although we do have many women business leaders, in India women are viewed with more empathy than men, even in the corporate world. The adage "Women can get things done with a smile" is sometimes true!

Laine (Philippines): People may take a less strong or softer approach when dealing with women counterparts out of traditional respect, but this is becoming less the case as women take on bigger roles. This is a reflection that women are increasingly being seen and treated as equals.

Paulo (Brazil): There are no differences between men and women in the workplace. Women should be focused on business and will be respected like all men. There are few women who take leadership in Brazil, but it is becoming more and more common.

CLOSING WORDS OF ADVICE

I asked the panelists if they had any additional words of advice for my U.S. executive. Here are their replies:

Judette (Trinidad and Tobago): The main "beef" with American businesspeople is their tendency to come over as arrogant and closed and to run roughshod over others. Relationships matter when doing business in T&T—invest the time in getting to know the culture, showing an openness to it. Don't just hang out with fellow Americans because that is your comfort zone. And be prepared to loosen up a little. Go to the local liming spots (neighborhood bars, clubs, and restaurants), join the Cricket Club, and show that you are not always so intense.

Sujit (India): As India is a very family oriented, affable society, good trustworthy relationships play an important role when doing business, and things work out faster if a relation of trust is built. My recommendation would be to have a consistent positive forward-looking emotion even if one does not get the business one hoped for, as there is always a next time.

Roberto (Mexico): Latin American culture is based on relationships and not business. In any meeting, 60 percent of the time will be spent in "How's the family? How's business? What do you think about the current situation?" Once everyone is relaxed, you talk business. People who approach business first without concern for personal matters usually fail in Mexico. There are always exceptions, but this is generally how I see it.

Silvia (Germany): Germany is a large country. Southern Germany is very different from the north (Catholic South vs. Protestant North, and so on)—and East Germany, which used to be part of the Socialist bloc, has its own unique history. When preparing for a meeting, try to understand these differences. Appreciate historical backgrounds and honor experiences that might contradict your way of looking at life.

Do the Right Thing

Greetings

UK/Irish Republic: men and women—a handshake

Brazil/S. America: men and women—a handshake; with friends, a hug or kiss

Australia: men and women—a firm handshake

Mexico/Latin America: a handshake initially; when more familiar, men hug, women kiss

Germany: men and women—a firm, determined, no-nonsense handshake, with eye contact to match

Western Europe generally (France, Italy, Spain, Low Countries, and so on): a friendly, not-quite-so-determined handshake, with friendly eye contact

UAE/Middle East (generally): men and women— a handshake; a kiss between women who know one another well

Saudi Arabia and some other Middle Eastern countries: a slight bow, sometimes with hand on heart—no handshake; if in doubt, watch others

Japan/China/Far East generally: men and women—a handshake; if both parties are Asian, a bow, if preferred; modest eye contact

India: men and women—a firm, warm handshake

Africa (Central and Southern generally): men and women—a handshake

North Africa generally: men and women—see Middle East, above

The Philippines: men and women—a firm handshake

Business Cards

UK/Irish Republic: seldom exchanged, except to provide contact info if not otherwise available or if, in future, one-to-one contact will be required

Brazil/S. America: not handed out usually, but often laid on the conference table to assist in identifying everyone

Australia: not handed out indiscriminately—only in cases of important relationships

Mexico/Latin America: usually handed out during the greeting

Germany: treated with great importance; often used to check if your title matches your company status

Western Europe generally: less formal; used for contact info mainly (Italians sometimes don't bother—which drives Germans crazy!)

UAE/Middle East generally: handed out formally during greetings for identification purposes

Japan/China/Far East: *very* important as part of the formal greeting; also important to treat received cards with respect and interest

India: again, formal exchange of cards very important

Africa: handed round at the beginning of a meeting

The Philippines: important

Time

UK/Irish Republic: For meetings, arriving five to eight minutes late is just about okay if unavoidable. Fifteen minutes late is rude. Meetings may overrun by fifteen minutes, so tailor your next appointments accordingly.

Brazil/S. America: Time is no big deal in Latin America. Meetings may begin up to thirty minutes late—and stop times are almost unheard of. Try to be on time for one-on-one meetings, though.

Australia: Be on time for meetings—even if they start a few minutes late.

Mexico/Latin America: See Brazil.

Germany: Arrive early. (It shows enthusiasm!) You won't be lonely—your German colleagues will have arrived early, too.

Western Europe generally: Try to be on time for meetings. If you have an excuse, a few minutes late is okay. But, as in the UK, more than a few is rude.

UAE/Middle East generally: Typical of the mysterious Middle East, it is bad manners to arrive late for meetings, though meetings never start on time.

Japan/China/Far East: In Japan, meetings tend to start on or nearly on time, but may overrun by as much as an hour. In China, time seems to play no controlling role at all—meetings are often convened at a few minutes' notice, and end when they end. Nobody seems bothered by this, though—and believe me, business does get done!

India: Despite the notorious Indian Standard Time (IST), meetings tend to start within ten to fifteen minutes of the scheduled time—but very often end when the chair decides there is no more business to do.

Africa: In general, arrive five minutes early if you want to be taken seriously.

The Philippines: Arrive on time—or nearly—but expect to wait up to thirty minutes for meetings to begin.

Space

UK/Irish Republic: Stand about two feet apart. No touching.

Brazil/S. America: Stand wherever you feel comfortable. Touching is fine.

Australia: Don't be fooled by the laid-back rep. *Crocodile Dundee* is only a movie. Aussies, in fact, are rather straitlaced folk. Three to four feet apart is comfortable standing space, and there is definitely no touching.

Mexico/Latin America: Two feet apart or closer is appropriate; touching is okay.

Germany: Arm's length apart is appropriate; there is no touching.

W. Europe generally: Stand two feet apart. Touching in some countries is normal, but watch the others for cues.

UAE/Middle East: Stand as close as you like, but there should be no touching.

Japan/China/Far East: Stand three to four feet apart in Japan, and there should be no touching. In China, stand two feet apart, or closer if it's comfortable. Touching is not common social practice, but okay as a way to show trust.

India: Stand two feet apart. Some touching is okay to show friendship or trust.

Africa: Stand two feet apart; there should be minimal or no touching.

The Philippines: Stand two feet apart. Touching is generally seen as inappropriate.

Eye Contact

UK/Irish Republic: Eye contact should not be too direct for too long, especially with Brits, who tend to feel they're being watched rather than looked at.

Brazil/S. America: The more eye contact, the more confident and honest you appear to be.

Australia: Lack of eye contact makes you seem untrustworthy. Constant eye contact, however, causes unease.

Mexico/Latin America: See Brazil.

Germany: Don't flinch! Flinchers can't be trusted.

W. Europe generally: Maintain steady eye contact. Keep it friendly.

UAE/Middle East: Reasonable eye contact suggests honesty and seriousness. Anything like staring, however, is considered rude.

Japan/China/Far East: In Japan, minimal eye contact is considered proper. Too much indicates a negative or even hostile response to colleagues. In China, it's best to avoid direct eye contact. Looking straight into another person's eyes is impolite.

India: Emphatic eye contact indicates trust and confidence. Prolonged staring, however, is discourteous, especially with female colleagues.

Africa: Modest eye contact is the best policy.

The Philippines: Eye contact shows interest and sincerity.

Emotion

UK/Irish Republic: Normal emotion is perfectly acceptable—not too much passion, however.

Shouting is always read as weakness. Wit, irony, a bit of sarcasm are all valued. Tears are not, however. Curiously, the more detached one appears to be, the more powerfully one comes across.

Brazil/S. America: Friendly, emotional talk about family, friends, and personal lives will usually be the starting point for conferences, seminars, and so on. Being open emotionally is a way of demonstrating friendliness, interest, and seriousness.

Australia: Emotional neutrality is the key here. Emotional display of any kind makes Australians feel uncomfortable and makes you seem limited.

Mexico/Latin America: See Brazil.

Germany: Power displays, even anger and verbal attacks, are tactically normal in negotiations and meetings. Yell back, and you'll be respected. Look uneasy, and they'll think there's something wrong with you.

W. Europe generally: Yelling and crying aren't good moves. Friendliness, banter, and a little warmth are fine. Nearly all Europeans speak some English, and many speak it very well—including the Germans—so expect to get as good as you give.

UAE/Middle East: Always behave politely without being standoffish. Emotion and personal relations play a central role in Middle Eastern business. But never lose your temper or make rude gestures—you could end up in jail.

Japan/China/Far East: The Chinese can become quite animated and even loud in business meetings. Laughing, yelling, and so on are not considered rude. In Japan, they are. Emotional display is considered unseemly there. Elsewhere in the Far East, emotional customs differ considerably. So simply be polite and quietly spoken and take your cues from the others.

India: Be politely friendly. Keep the emotional level down.

Africa: Stay calm and cool.

The Philippines: Be polite. Keep your emotions under control without being aloof.

9

THE NONVERBAL FUTURE OF LEADERSHIP

New Generations and New Technology

Kendra is majoring in corporate strategic planning in the Business Finance Department of one of the top U.S. universities. With one semester of schooling to complete, Kendra spent the summer as an intern in one of the leading high-tech companies in Silicon Valley. That company just made her an offer for full-time employment after graduation, which Kendra will accept—unless she gets the counteroffer she's hoping for, from one of the world's most prestigious management consulting firms.

Kendra is an example of top talent—one of the best and the brightest of a new generation of workers who are the future of your organization. Your ability to attract, retain, and engage the Kendras (and Kenneths) of this generation will, in a large part, determine whether your organization will continue to thrive or must struggle to stay competitive in the years ahead.

Your organization will change this group of workers—building their capabilities, molding their talents, guiding them from the theoretical base of their educations to the practical realities of your business. In turn, your new workforce will change the structure and spirit of your organization with its creativity, energy, adaptability, and enthusiasm.

In previous chapters, we've looked at the increasingly global and multicultural makeup of the workforce, seen how leading-edge communication technologies are changing business practices, and noted the fact that, in the United States, women are now the majority of employees. In this chapter, you will learn the ways that each generation of workers brings change to the organization, the values and expectations of the newest workers, the amazing potential of technological innovation, and how all these factors point the way toward a more collaborative and inclusive leadership style. Then we'll close by summarizing the future of nonverbal communication and why body language acumen will be an increasingly crucial aspect of leadership effectiveness.

ALL GENERATIONS BRING CHANGE

My father worked thirty-five years for the *San Francisco Examiner* newspaper. He loved to talk about his work, but never once did he mention his company's vision, mission statement, or corporate values. That's because the command-and-control, military model of leadership he served under didn't see the need for that kind of "soft stuff." And for my father's generation of workers, who had been raised during the Great Depression of the early 1930s and felt lucky to have any job, this was a perfectly acceptable arrangement.

Of course, the Baby Boomers (born between 1946 and 1964) changed that. Seventy-eight million strong, they came into the workforce looking for meaning, empowerment, and engagement—and before we knew it, every organization looking to attract and retain the top talent of this generation was busy creating mission, vision, and values statements. The "flower power" generation, many of whom had marched, rallied, and lobbied for women's and minority rights, pushed that agenda into corporate boardrooms and organizational policies. And because Boomers wanted more face-to-face interaction and were less responsive to directives, management began to evolve into "servant leadership" and "transformational leadership" models.

The increased birth control and career options offered to Boomer women resulted in the much smaller generation that followed. Born between 1965 and 1983, Generation X didn't have the clout of large numbers, but they did have a unique and advantageous skill set: they were technologically savvy at a time when technology (most especially the Internet) was beginning to change business practices in substantial ways. Their economic timing was good too. They entered the job market during the dot-com boom, so their demands for cappuccino machines, pets at work, and free massages were met—and exceeded—by organizations eager to compete in the "war for talent."

They brought other changes as well. Where Boomers wanted face-to-face interaction with their managers, Gen Xers preferred e-mail and intranet communication. Where Boomers thought they had signed up with their employers for the long term, Gen Xers knew differently. In response to the demise of the organizational retention agreement, this generation redefined commitment in shorter terms—and turned job hopping into the new career path.

Now, another generation is entering the workforce. Pierced, tattooed, digital, networked, and mobile— Generation Y is like nothing your organization has seen before. And, as did their predecessors, they will bring their own unique set of capabilities, challenges, and changes.

THE NEW GENERATION OF WORKERS

Generation Y comprises those individuals born between 1984 and 2002. In some circles they're called Millennials, and in numbers they rival the Baby Boomer genera- tion. Today's Gen Yers come to the workplace with a markedly different perspective than those of past generations. Having grown up under the guidance of parents positioning them for success, they recognize the potential to make a significant impact in the business world. At the same time, as eyewitnesses to the corporate and institutional scandals of recent years, they are highly skeptical of authority. And, as a generation that marketers have targeted their entire lives, they are also highly resistant to the pumped-up "happy talk" of corporate leaders.

They have in common many other shared experiences that will create bonds among them—and distinguish them from your current workers. Consider, for example, that television was the defining technology for Baby Boomers and drove a culture of homogeneity. For this new generation, the defining technology has been the Internet, which drives diversity.

They have a high tolerance for change and innovation and aren't afraid of being fired; they're more afraid of being bored. The college graduates among them don't expect to stay with their first employer for more than two years. They have been told they will have many jobs in a variety of organizations over the course of several different careers.

They represent the most racially and ethnically diverse generation in history. They come, as well, from a different social and cultural environment than past generations: one in three Millennials is non-Caucasian, one in four is from a single-parent home, and three in four have working mothers. They are hitting the workplace just as the Baby Boom generation reaches retirement. They are super ready for employment in your organization. But are you ready for them?

GEN Y AND THE FUTURE OF VISUAL TECHNOLOGY

According to a study by Cisco Systems, more than 50 percent of Gen Y own a webcam, and 20 percent visit YouTube multiple times a day.[1] They are more likely to have their own social networking profiles and to post videos of themselves online than are older generations. This preference for visual media has already changed employee interactions and knowledge sharing in many organizations. In the past, information was primarily shared via text documents, e-mail, and PowerPoint slides, but now employees are increasingly filming short videos to share best practices with colleagues and to brief peers about projects and initiatives. (One current example is Microsoft, which offers free podcasting equipment to all employees who agree to create three knowledge-sharing videos a year. The entries are then posted on Academy Mobile, on Microsoft's intranet.)

But when it comes to unleashing the full power of visual technology, we haven't seen anything yet! Here are three examples that could change the way your entire business operates: a new product, a research project, and a technology demonstration—IVN's

Silhouette, Project LifeLike, and Cisco's holographic
version of TelePresence.

Silhouette

You show up for work at company headquarters. You
attend a meeting in one of the conference rooms, but
find that the topic under discussion doesn't concern
you, so you exit that room and visit a colleague's office
to collaborate on a project you've both been assigned to.
Before you leave for the day, you check with the head of
human resources about a personnel issue.

Oh—did I mention that you do all of this (from any-
where in the world) on your personal computer?

Blending a 3-D online environment (in this case, a
virtual building with offices and meeting rooms) with live
streaming video with synchronized audio, IVN's Silhouette
offers a new and unique option for a distributed workforce
to meet "face-to-face" in a virtual world. Silhouette is the
first technology that allows users to be totally immersed in
a 3-D world each via his or her actual image.

Silhouette takes her from home office to virtual boardroom.

Silhouette represents a significant advance, as it allows participants to be "placed" in a virtual environment and yet see each other as live video images (instead of computer-generated "cartoon" avatars). And this is all done over the Web at real-time frame rates with fully synchronized audio. So no special equipment is necessary. Silhouette uses a standard-issue webcam to extract the user's image, which is then "transported" to the virtual company location to attend meetings, collaborate, or otherwise interact with other participants.

Silhouette is a new product, but already it has attracted the attention of organizations like IBM, Microsoft, Intel, Cisco, Google, and Disney, as well as the U.S. Government.

Project LifeLike

Project LifeLike is a collaboration between the Intelligent Systems Laboratory at the University of Central Florida and the Electronic Visualization Laboratory at the University of Illinois at Chicago. The project aims to create avatars that are ... well, lifelike.

Beyond trying to create characters that actually look like real people (instead of some cartoon-like representations), researchers are also finding ways to incorporate body language cues in the interchanges. With sensors connected to individuals, researchers track and replicate facial expressions, eye movements, and gestures in order to give avatars the ability to express emotional signals, to read those same nuances in people, and to adjust their communication accordingly.

Businesswoman and her more life-like avatar

Although the current results are far from perfect replications of specific individuals, this work has greatly advanced the field and opened up a host of possible new refinements for application in the not-too-distant future. If you've ever wanted to create a copy of yourself that could stand in for you at a meeting, freeing you up to work on more pressing matters, you may be closer than you think to getting your wish.

Soon it may be possible for global employees sitting at their computers to meet online for a conversation with avatars of corporate leaders, or for job seekers to hone their interview skills by practicing with an avatar. In fact, in the coming decades, many of the "people" you interact with may not actually be people at all. But you can bet that they will be masters of nonverbal communication!

Avatars with Body Language Skills

In a Stanford University experiment using a computer-animated sales agent, the mimicry of an individual's head movement made the avatar seem both more honest and more persuasive.[2]

Holographic TelePresence

It was only a demonstration, but the Cisco TelePresence On-Stage Experience (a collaboration between Cisco and Musion Systems) took place during the opening of Cisco's Globalization Centre East and created the world's first live holographic video feed from San Jose, California, to Bangalor, India. It wowed the audience—and gave the rest of us a glimpse into the future of visual technology.

Cisco CEO John Chambers, who was live on the Bangalore stage, "beamed up" Marthin De Beer, the senior vice president of emerging technologies, and Chuck Stucki, the general manager of TelePresence, live from San Jose. Chambers was then able to have a face-to-face discussion with the holographic De Beer and Stucki on the future of Cisco TelePresence, demonstrating the potential capabilities of the system in front of the watching audience.

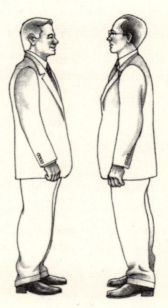

One of these men is a hologram.

This demonstration showed the audience how Cisco's TelePresence plans to move from a 2-D immersive solution into a 3-D immersive solution mimicking

Star Trek–like situations with holograms. It is Cisco's prediction that holographic meetings will be replacing videoconferencing in the near future.

If all goes as planned, 3-D holographic conferencing will first be used at large expositions and conferences and will then trickle down to corporate use. At that time, a sales manager would be able to virtually walk into a client's office and have a detailed conversation—with his or her holographic image traveling overseas to the remotest countries via an Internet connection. A CEO could address an entire employee population and announce a new strategy—and the audience could see the executive's full range of nonverbal communication, as if he or she were there in person.

THE FUTURE OF LEADERSHIP

The twenty-first century is seeing the bringing together of new employees, new technologies, and new global business realities that adds up to one word: collaboration. New workers will demand it, advances in technology will enable it, and, in addition, the "borderless organization" of the future will dictate that future productivity gains can only be achieved by creating collaborative teams that are networked to span corporate and national boundaries.

With new business realities comes a new leadership model—one that replaces command and control with transparency and inclusion. The leader's new role will be to encourage employees to see themselves as empowered and valued contributors—and to help them build their knowledge base and expand their personal networks. To fulfill this role, leaders can no longer permit themselves the luxury of issuing orders from ivory towers. They must descend to the front line, become coaches and team players willing to get in the trenches and work side by side with other team members. They must demonstrate a greater degree of emotional intelligence—and be able to show they understand, support, and care about the people in their charge. The success of this collaborative approach to leadership will rely far more heavily on what leaders do than on what they say.

Which brings us to the importance of body language as an essential skill set for future leadership success.

PREDICTIONS FOR THE FUTURE OF BODY LANGUAGE

Leaders who really do feel more comfortable in an ivory tower may soon have to make the following decision about their futures: either agree to step down from their comfort zones—or simply step down. Why? Here's why:

Prediction One: The visual technology revolution will make body language skills even more crucial than they are today.

There is no doubt that videoconferencing that allows participants to see one another can help build stronger bonds and improve rapport. But video communication can also heighten a participant's anxiety and self-consciousness because there is no hiding behind a text message or computer screen.

Leaders have always been under scrutiny, but with the future developments in multimedia technology, a leader's body language is even more exposed to evaluation. Leaders will need to develop the verbal and nonverbal skills to make the most of these new tools.

Prediction Two: A young generation of "leaders-in-training" may need additional training in nonverbal communication.

You know that technology is changing our lives. But did you know that it is also changing our brains? According to Gary Small, director of UCLA's Memory and Aging Research Center, this is true for everyone, but it is most relevant for the "digital natives"—those younger employees who were born into a world of laptops and cell phones, text messaging and twittering, and who have been accused of spending too much time (over eight hours a day) using technology and too little time engaging in direct social contact.[3]

Some of the resultant brain changes will have positive implications for future employers: the rewiring of neural circuitry is heightening such skills as the ability to pick out details amid clutter—which in turn enhances complex reasoning and decision making. But while the brain is developing circuitry for online social networking, it is also producing shortened attention spans and diminished social skills, including nonverbal communication skills and important emotional aptitudes like empathy.

All human beings are hardwired to understand body language, and the new workforce generation has the same innate ability, even if they may be missing some of the lessons that they could have picked up had they received more practice in handling face-to-face encounters. To build (or reinforce) their collaboration skills, many people in this generation will need coaching in the basics of nonverbal communication.

Prediction Three: The body language of effective leaders will become increasingly "warm."

I've talked previously about the two sets of body language cues that followers look for in leaders. One set projects warmth and empathy, and the other signals power and authority. Both are necessary for leaders today, and both will be critical to the success of leaders in the future. But if your organization is headed toward a collaborative structure and philosophy, then effective leadership becomes less about projecting power and more about building relationships. And relationship building, in turn, is all about the body language of trust, inclusion, and rapport. So the "soft side" of nonverbal communication (which has been undervalued and underutilized by leaders more concerned with projecting strength, status, and authority) will become central to achieving your business goals.

Prediction Four: Body language research will focus more on business and leadership applications.

I receive updates every day as people in the fields of neuroscience, social science, psychology, and information technology continue to research and validate nonverbal communication in business and leadership. To keep you up-to-date with what I'm continuing to learn, and to reinforce the skills you've already acquired, I've designed my Web site www.SilentLanguageOfLeaders.com with videos, articles, and links to other resources, and I invite you to contact me at CGoman@CKG.com with any question, comment, or request.

Prediction Five: Authenticity will be increasingly revealed through body language.

One of the most prominent authorities on organization development and leadership was speaking at a conference I attended. An audience member asked the leadership guru if he had ever made the following statement: "Leadership is 85 percent character." The speaker paused and answered, "Probably. But I'd change that now. Leadership is 100 percent character."

Body language reveals character. Regardless of how skilled a nonverbal communicator he or she is, no leader can fool the people who work with him or her over an extended period of time. Sooner or later, your body will give you away. Like good manners and good grammar, body language is a tool for expressing your "best" self in a certain situation. And it is a highly valuable tool. It just can't hide your character.

You can become aware of and change ineffective body language habits; you can develop a deeper understanding of the impact that certain nonverbal behaviors have on your audiences; and you can add more effective gestures, postures, and expressions to your leadership repertoire. But the most charismatic, influential, and powerful body language will always be that which is totally congruent with who you are, what you stand for, and what you truly believe.

ACKNOWLEDGMENTS

I am deeply indebted to Marc Wright, Paulo Soares, Helen Wang, Judette Coward-Puglisi, Jennifer Frahm, Roberto Islas, Silvia Cambié, Priya Sarma, Kazuhiro Amemiya, Sujit Patil, Saada Ibrahim Mufuruki, and Laine Santana, who took time from their busy schedules to share their experiences of nonverbal communication practices in global business meetings. And I owe special thanks to Gretchen Hoover Anderson (vice president of global membership, marketing, and development at the International Association of Business Communicators) for her help in identifying and contacting these contributors.

I am so very grateful to George Kimball for editing this book. I looked forward to his comments on each chapter—and loved how the book got better and better as a result of his suggestions.

I want to acknowledge the dedicated "tag-team" at Jossey-Bass (Genoveva Llosa, Byron Schneider, and Gayle Mak) for their guidance, encouragement, and support.

I also want to thank Joe Tessitore, who believed in this book from the beginning and who represented it so admirably.

And, last, I want to express my appreciation to Pat Welch of Chameleon Design for all his artistic efforts (Web site design, book illustrations, and so on) on my behalf. I know I am in good and talented hands when working with him.

NOTES

INTRODUCTION

1. Pentland, A. (2008). *Honest signals: How they shape our world.* Cambridge, MA: MIT Press.
2. Tsukiura, T., & Cabeza, R. (2008). *Orbitofrontal and hippocampal contributions to memory for face-name associations: The rewarding power of a smile.* Unedited manuscript published online. www.ncbi.nlm.nih.gov/pmc/articles/PMC2517599.

CHAPTER ONE: LEADERSHIP AT A GLANCE

1. Keim, B. (2008, April). Brain scanners can see decisions before you make them. *Wired.* www.wired.com/science/discoveries/news/2008/04/mind_decision.
2. Tracy, J. L., & Matsumoto, D. (2008). The spontaneous expression of pride and shame: Evidence for biologically innate nonverbal displays. *Proceedings of the National Academy of Sciences, 105,* 11655–11660.
3. Westen, D. (2007). *The political brain: The role of emotion in deciding the fate of the nation.* New York: PublicAffairs, p. 294.
4. Ambady, N., & Rosenthal, R. (2000). Thin slices of expressive behavior as predictors of interpersonal consequences: A meta-analysis. *Psychological Bulletin, 111,* 256–274.
5. Amabile, T. (1983, March). Brilliant but cruel: Perceptions of negative evaluators. *Journal of Experimental Social Psychology, 19,* 146–156.

6. Goman, C. K. (2008). *The nonverbal advantage: Secrets and science of body language at work.* San Francisco: Berrett-Koehler, pp. 17–18.
7. Thorndike, E. L. (1920). A constant error on psychological rating. *Journal of Applied Science, 82,* 665–674.
8. Project Implicit. Implicit Associations Test (IAT). https://implicit.harvard.edu/implicit/.
9. Kelly, S. D., Kravitz, C., & Hopking, M. (2004). Neural correlates of bimodal speech and gesture comprehension. *Brain and Language, 89,* 253–260.

CHAPTER TWO: NEGOTIATION

1. Pentland, A. (2008, Fall). Understanding "honest signals" in business. *MIT Sloan Management Review, 50*(1), 70–75.
2. Stark, P. (2004). Become a master negotiator. Everyone Negotiates. www.everyonenegotiates.com/newsletter/archive/Master%20Negotiator%20issue%209.htm.
3. Nierenberg, G., & Calero, H. (1971). *How to read a person like a book.* New York: Pocket Books, p. 56.
4. Temple-Raston, D. (2007, October). Neuroscientist uses brain scan to see lies form. NPR. www.npr.org/templates/story/story.php?storyId=15744871.

CHAPTER THREE: LEADING CHANGE

1. Goleman, D. (2002). *The new leaders: Transforming the art of leadership into the science of results.* London: Sphere, p. 3.
2. Damasio, A. (2009). This time with feeling. FORA.tv interview. http://fora.tv/2009/07/04/Antonio_Damasio_This_Time_With_Feeling#fullprogramFORA.tv.
3. Barsade, S. (2001, August). The ripple effect: Emotional contagion in groups. *Yale School of Management Working Paper Series,* OB-01. http://papers.ssrn.com/abstract=250894.
4. Restak, R. (2006). *The naked brain: How the emerging neurosociety is changing how we live, work, and love.* New York: Three Rivers Press, p. 103.
5. Davis, S. F., & Palladino, J. J. (2000). *Psychology* (3rd ed.). Upper Saddle River, NJ: Prentice-Hall.

6. Ekman, P. (1983). Autonomic nervous system activity distinguishes among emotions. *Science, 221*(4616), 1208–1210.

7. Koch, S., Holland R., Hengstler M., & van Knippenberg, A. (2009). Body locomotion as regulatory process: Stepping backward enhances cognitive control. *Psychological Science, 20,* 549–550.

8. Hanna, J. (2010, September 20). Power posing: Fake it until you make it. *Harvard Business School Working Knowledge.* http://hbswk.hbs.edu/item/6461.html.

9. Moorehead, M. V. (1992, February 26). Is acting really in your blood? Scientists check out a dramatic clue to good health. *Phoenix NewTimes.* www.phoenixnewtimes.com/1992-02-26/news/is-acting-really-in-your-blood-local-scientists-check-out-a-dramatic-clue-to-good-health/.

10. Gross, J. (2000, July 6). Emotion lab. *Quantum.* ABC Television. www.abc.net.au/quantum/stories/s146172.htm.

11. Sanfey, A., Rilling, J., Aronson, J., Nystrom, L., & Cohen, J. (2003, June). The neural basis of economic decision-making in the ultimatum game. *Science, 300*(5626), 1755–1758.

CHAPTER FOUR: COLLABORATION

1. Eisenberger, N. I., Lieberman, M. D., & Williams, K. D. (2003). Does rejection hurt? An fMRI study of social exclusion. *Science, 302*(5643), 290–292.

2. Mother Teresa quotes. BrainyQuotes. www.brainyquote.com/quotes/authors/m/mother_teresa_2.html.

3. Poster presented at the 14th conference of the International Society for Research on Emotions, Bari, Italy, July 11–15, 2005.

4. Van baaren, R. B., Holland, R. W., Kawakami, K., & van Kippenberg, A. (2009). Mimicry and prosocial behavior. *Psychological Science, 15*(1), 71–74.

5. Wiltermuth, S. S., & Heath, C. (2009). Synchrony and cooperation. *Psychological Science, 20*(1). www.glocha.info/glocha350/images/stories/pdf/wiltermuth-2009-music_evolution_synchrony_cooperation.pdf.

6. Beukeboom, C. (2008, September). When words feel right: How affective expressions of listeners change a speaker's

language use. *European Journal of Social Psychology, 39,* 747–756.

7. Rhem, J. (1999, February). Pygmalion in the classroom. *National Teaching & Learning Forum, 8*(2). www.ntlf.com/html/pi/9902/pygm_1.htm.

8. Riggio, R. (2009, April). Pygmalion leadership: The power of positive expectations. *Psychology Today.* www.psychologytoday .com/blog/cutting-edge-leadership/200904/pygmalion-leadership-the-power-positive-expectations.

9. Grifantini, K. (2009, March 11). Making robots give the right glances. *Technology Review.* www.technologyreview.com/computing/22271/?a=f.

10. Ambady, N., Laplante, D., Nguyen, T., Rosenthal, R., Chaumeton, N., & Levinson, W. (2002, July). Surgeons' tone of voice: A clue to malpractice history. *Surgery, 132*(1), 5–9.

11. Ethofer, T., Van De Vill, D., Scherer, K., & Vuilleumier, P. (2009, June 23). Decoding of emotional information in voice-sensitive cortices. *Current Biology, 19,* 1028–1033.

12. Marmot, M. (2004). *The status syndrome: How social standing affects our health and longevity.* New York: Owl Books.

13. Kunst-Wilson, W. R., & Zajonc, R. B. (1980). Affective discrimination of stimuli that cannot be recognized. *Science, 207*(4430), 557–558.

CHAPTER FIVE: COMMUNICATING VIRTUALLY AND FACE-TO-FACE

1. Lojeski, K. (2009). *When distance matters: An overview of virtual distance.* White paper posted on www.virtualdistance.com.

2. Kruger, J., Epley, N., Parker, J., & Ng, Z. -W. (2005). Egocentrism over e-mail: Can we communicate as well as we think? *Journal of Personality and Social Psychology, 89,* 925–936.

3. Pearn Kandola. (2006, September). The psychology of effective business communications in geographically dispersed teams. *News@Cisco.* http://newsroom.cisco.com.

4. Medina, J. (2008, March 16). The brain cannot multitask. Brain Rules. http://brainrules.blogspot.com/2008/03/brain-cannot-multitask_16.html.

5. Ferran, C., & Watts, S. (2008, September). Videoconferencing in the field: A heuristic processing model. *Management Science, 54*, 1565–1578.

6. van Wassenhove, V., Skipper, J., Nusbaum, H. C., & Small, S. (2007). Hearing lips and seeing voices: How cortical areas supporting speech production mediate audiovisual speech perception. *Cerebral Cortex, 17*, 2387–2399.

7. IBM. *IBM virtual world guidelines.* http://domino.research.ibm .com/comm/research_projects.nsf/pages/virtualworlds.IBM VirtualWorldGuidelines.html.

8. Yee, N., & Bailenson, J. (2007). The Proteus effect: The effect of transformed self-representation on behavior. *Human Communication Research, 33*, 271–290.

9. Harvard Business Review Analytic Services. (n.d.). Managing across distance in today's economic climate: The value of face-to-face communication. *Harvard Business Review.* http://hkg.grants.ba.com/harvard-business-review.pdf.

10. Phone interview with Terry Pearce, April 22, 2010.

11. Lewis, T., & Lannon, R. (2000). *A general theory of love.* New York: Random House, pp. 35–65.

12. Goman, C. K. (2004). *This isn't the company I joined: How to lead in a business turned upside down.* Berkeley, CA: KCS Publishing, pp. 169–170.

13. Scafidi, F. A., Field, T. M., Schanberg, S. M., Bauer, C. R., Tucci, K., Roberts, J., Morrow, C., & Kuhn, C. M. (1990). Massage stimulates growth in preterm infants: A replication. *Infant Behavior and Development, 13*, 167–188.

14. Carey, B. (2010, February 23). Evidence that little touches do mean so much. *New York Times.* www.nytimes.com/ 2010/02/23/health/23mind.html.

15. Geddes, D. (1998, July 9). CU study: Restaurant customers give better tips to server with touch. *Cornell Chronicle.* www.news.cornell.edu/chronicle/98/7.9.98/touch_study .html.

16. Hertenstein, M., & Keltner, D. (2006). Touch communicates distinct emotions. *American Psychological Association, 6*(3), 528–533.

CHAPTER SIX: HE LEADS, SHE LEADS

1. University of California, Irvine. (2005, January 22). Intelligence in men and women is a gray and white matter. *ScienceDaily*. www.sciencedaily.com/releases/2005/01/050121100142.htm.

2. Brizendine, L. (2010). *The male brain*. New York: Broadway Books, pp. 96–98.

3. Marcozzi, G., Liberati, V., Madia, F., Centofanti, M., & de Feo, G. (2003). Age- and gender-related differences in human lacrimal fluid peroxidase activity. *Opthalmologica, 217*, 294–297.

4. Wang, J., Korczykowski, M., Rao, H., Fan, Y., Pluta, J., Gur, R. C., McEwen, B. S., & Detre, J. A. *Gender differences in neural response to psychological stress*. Center for Functional Neuroimaging, University of Pennsylvania. www.cfn.upenn.edu/perfusion/stress.pdf.

5. Wickelgren, I. (2010, April 19). Under threat, women bond, men withdraw. *Scientific American*. http://scientificamerican.com/article.cfm?id=under-threat-women-bond.

6. Butler, D., & Geis, F. L. (1990). Nonverbal affect responses to male and female leaders: Implications for leadership evaluations. *Journal of Personality and Social Psychology, 58*(1), 48–59.

7. Rosenthal, R., Archer, D., Koivumaki, J. H., DiMatteo, M. R., & Rogers, P. L. (1974, January). Assessing sensitivity to nonverbal communication: The PONS test. *Division 8 Newsletter* (Division of Personality and Social Psychology of the American Psychological Association), pp. 1–3.

8. Brescoll, V., & Uhlmann, E. L. (2008). Can an angry woman get ahead? *Psychological Science, 19*, 268–275.

9. Clark, N. (2009, June 15). An interview with Madeleine Albright. *Women's Media*. www.womensmedia.com/work/131-an-interview-with-madeleine-albright.html.

10. Academy of Management. (2008, July). Flirting is a money loser in negotiations, new research finds. Press release. Academy of Management. www.aomonline.org/aom.asp?ID=251&page_ID=224&pr_id=398.

CHAPTER SEVEN: WORKING WITH GLOBAL TEAMS

1. Hall, E. T. (1976). *Beyond culture*. Garden City, NY: Anchor Press/Doubleday.

2. Chen, M. -J. (2001). *Inside Chinese business: A guide for managers worldwide*. Boston: Harvard Business School Press, p. 94.

3. Johnson, C. Y. (2008, August 18). The winners' body language—it's biological. *Boston Globe*. www.boston.com/sports/other_sports/olympics/articles/2008/.

4. Ekman, P. (2003). *Emotions revealed*. New York: Owl Books.

5. Matsumoto, D. Subtle expression recognition training. Humintell. www.humintell.com/subtle-expression-recognition-training/.

6. Ekman, P. (1992). *Telling lies*. New York: Norton.

CHAPTER NINE: THE NONVERBAL FUTURE OF LEADERSHIP

1. Cisco Systems. (2010, February 23). Cisco retail banking survey finds Generation Y consumers' needs will transform retail banking. Press release. http://newsroom.cisco.com/dlls/2010/prod_022310.html.

2. Bailson, J., & Yee, N. (2005, October). Digital chameleons: Automatic assimilation of nonverbal gestures in immersive virtual environments. *Psychological Science, 16*, 814–819.

3. Lin, J. (2008, October 15). Research shows that Internet is rewiring our brains. *UCLAToday—Faculty and Staff News*. www.today.ucla.edu/portal/ut/081015_gary-small-ibrain.aspx.

ABOUT THE AUTHOR

Carol Kinsey Goman, Ph.D., president of Kinsey Consulting Services (KCS), is a leadership coach, management consultant, keynote speaker, and seminar leader for corporations, associations, and government agencies. Clients include over one hundred organizations in twenty-four countries—corporate giants, such as Consolidated Edison, Royal Bank of Canada, and PepsiCo; major nonprofit organizations, such as the American Institute of Banking, the Healthcare Forum, and the American Society of Training and Development; high-tech firms, such as Cisco, Hewlett-Packard, and Texas Instruments; membership organizations, such as the Young Presidents' Organization and the Conference Board; government agencies, such as the Office of the Comptroller of the Currency, U.S. Army Tank-automotive and Armaments Command, and the Library of Congress; and international firms, such as Petroleos de Venezuela, Dairy Farm in Hong Kong, and Wartsilla Diesel in Finland.

Body language has always played a key role in Carol's professional life. Prior to founding KCS, she was a therapist in private practice—reading nonverbal cues to help clients make rapid and profound behavioral changes. Today, as an executive coach, Carol helps leaders build powerful and productive business relationships by using body language that projects confidence, credibility, warmth, and empathy.

Carol has an extensive background in organizational "people issues." She's published eleven books and more than three hundred articles in the fields of organizational change, leadership, communication, the multigenerational workforce, collaboration, employee engagement, and body language in the workplace. Carol is a human resource columnist for Troy Media and a frequent contributor to Forbes.com and the *Washington Post* "On Leadership" column. An upbeat and entertaining guest, she's been featured on radio and television shows including NPR's *Marketplace*, CNN's *Business Unusual*, ABC's *The View from the Bay*, and *NBC Nightly News*.

Carol has served as an adjunct faculty member at John F. Kennedy University in the International MBA program, at UC Berkeley in the Executive Education Department, and for the Chamber of Commerce of the United States at its Institutes for Organization Management. She is a current faculty member with the Institute for Management Studies.

Information about her programs and video clips of Carol can be found at www.SilentLanguageofLeaders.com and www.CKG.com.

INDEX